A SHORT AND HAPPY GUIDE TO CONTRACTS

By

David G. Epstein

George E. Allen Chair Professor of Law
University of Richmond

Bruce A. Markell

United States Bankruptcy Judge
District of Nevada
Senior Fellow, Bankruptcy and Commercial Law
William S. Boyd School of Law
University of Nevada, Las Vegas

Lawrence Ponoroff

Dean of the College & Samuel M. Fegtly
Chair in Commercial Law
The University of Arizona
James E. Rogers College of Law

WEST®

A Thomson Reuters business

Mat #41189299

© 2012 Thomson Reuters

610 Opperman Drive
St. Paul, MN 55123
1–800–313–9378

Printed in the United States of America

ISBN: 978–0–314–27793–0

Acknowledgements

We would like to thank Paula Franzese and Louis Higgins for making this book possible. Paula is an incredibly creative law professor who "invented" the Short and Happy series. Louis is our incredibly nice friend at West with even nicer daughters, Cecilia and Yvette.

And, Epstein would like to thank Juliet Moore who made this book better. Juliet, a law student at Georgetown, helped Epstein with his part of the book, and Epstein, bless his heart, needs all of the help he can get.

Ponoroff, although not being nearly as needy as Epstein, would like to thank Carol Lamoureux, an Arizona law student, who made several helpful suggestions from a student's perspective and did a fine editing job. He further wishes to acknowledge Alla Goldman, also an Arizona law student, who is responsible for the diagram of UCC § 2–207, which appears in Chapter 1 of the book.

Finally, and most important, we'd like to thank all of the professors assigned to teach contracts but who would have preferred to teach constitutional law (or to not teach at all so they could devote more time to their "scholarship")—they made this book necessary.

Introduction

Welcome to law school. In your first year, you'll have several courses, such as Civil Procedure, Torts, Criminal Law, and, of course, your most important course: Contracts. Why is Contracts so important? Just think about the last month. We're betting that during that time you did not: (1) sue anyone in federal court, (2) run down a pedestrian while driving under the influence, or (3) commit any major felonies. But we are willing to bet that during that same time you probably signed (1) an apartment lease, (2) an agreement for broadband wireless service, or (3) a promissory note for your student loans, and maybe all three. Each of those transactions, and perhaps several more in which you've engaged in the last month, involves a *contract*. So, as you can see, contract law pervades daily life from shelter to occupation to creature comforts.

Now, what does each of those "contracts" you may have entered into over the last month have in common? Each involved at least one *promise*. A promise, in its most elemental form, is an undertaking or commitment to do or not do something in the future. Generally speaking, a promise, once made, should be kept, right? But not all promises are equal in the eyes of the law; not every promise made can be enforced in a court of law. That's what contract law is all about—liability for promises, or, more accurately, broken promises. At its core, contract law is the system of rules and policies governing the legal enforcement of promises And, bear in mind, contract cases range from very simple deals, like those described above, to highly complex transactions, such as corporate mergers, technology transfer agreements, or construction financing arrangements, to name just a few.

In this book we will reveal those rules to you in as straightforward and clear a fashion as they permit. But we will also talk some about *policy* and the difference between the two. For now, think of them this way: policy reflects the normative objectives we want to attain, and the rules are the vehicles for getting us there. For example, one of the foundational policies behind contract law is that of "freedom of contract." That phrase refers to the right of a person to make a legally binding agreement with one or more other persons without governmental interference as to what type of obligations she can take upon herself or impose upon the other.

v

No policy, however, is absolute or without limitation. There are some areas where the law restricts the ability of private individuals to make a deal because of countervailing policy considerations. To use an extreme example, freedom of contract does not include the freedom of Epstein to enter into a contract with Markell to steal Ponoroff's huge royalties from sales of this book. Therefore, it is not inaccurate to think of the rules of contract law as mediating between achieving the principle favoring freedom of contract while not exceeding the restraints that society must necessarily place on that same freedom. Basically, the rules of contract law keep the ball in play.

Because not all promises can be enforced in court, each society must decide which promises it will legally enforce and which promises will be left to more informal incentives for compelling a party's performance, such as the promisor's conscience or concern for her reputation. For the most part, our legal system is concerned with promises that arise out of *exchange* transactions. So Epstein's promise to sell his car to Markell for $100 is typically enforceable, whereas Epstein's promise to *give* his car to Markell likely would not be. This tells you that contract law is most concerned with private bargains of exchange that transfer or allocate resources. Indeed, a free market economy depends on the predictable enforcement of private exchange transactions.

Most contract law is common law; which is to say, judge made law, developed over hundreds of years in individual cases. Contract law in this country was originally inherited from England at the time of the founding of the republic, and then continued to be developed by American courts. The early 20th Century saw the promulgation by the American Law Institute of *Restatements* of the law in several fields, including contracts. The *Restatements* are code-like documents that attempt to set out the law as it currently exists. They are influential, but without the force of law. In other words, a court is not bound to apply the *Restatement*. The first *Restatement of Contracts* was published in 1932, and the *Restatement (Second) of Contracts*, to which we will sometimes refer in this book, was approved in 1981. Generally speaking, the first *Restatement* reflected the more traditional or "classical" view of contract law, which favored hard and fast rules to resolve contract disputes in a predictable and consistent fashion. The *Restatement (Second)*, by contrast, is much less rule-bound. It adopts a more flexible approach; that is, one that emphasizes malleable standards over fixed and unbending rules, and encourages courts to take into account considerations external to the parties' contract in order to promote equity and fairness.

The middle of the 20th Century saw the adoption by its sponsoring agencies of the Uniform Commercial Code (the UCC), which is a model statute available to the states for enactment as law. Of importance for us, Article 2 of the UCC has been adopted by every state except for Louisiana. Article 2 governs contracts for the sale of goods; that is to say, moveable tangible things. Some provisions of Article 2 apply only to merchants—persons in the business of selling goods of the kind that are the subject of the contract—but Article 2 applies to *every* contract for the sale of goods, *even if* one or both parties are not merchants.

In this book, we are going to break the subject of contracts into seven short questions:

1. Has a deal been made?
2. Is the deal enforceable?
3. Are there defenses to enforcement of the deal?
4. What are the terms of the deal?
5. When will performance of the deal be excused?
6. How does the law enforce the deal?
7. Who else is affected by the deal?

Once you can answer these questions, you will have mastered contract law. We realize it seems a little daunting to you right now, but, hey, if the three of us could get through it, you'll do just fine. So, sit back and enjoy.

About the Authors

David G. Epstein, the "senior" co-author of this book, has taught Contracts at seven different law schools. For more than 30 years, he has also lectured on Contracts at bar review courses around the country. David now teaches at the University of Richmond Law School (which is wonderfully close to his sons' wonderful Charlottesville restaurant, Eppies) where he holds the George E. Allen Chair. (Created to honor an outstanding Virginia trial lawyer, not the former Redskins coach or his politically incorrect politician son).

Bruce A. Markell is a bankruptcy judge for the District of Nevada, and also serves on the Bankruptcy Appellate Panel for the Ninth Circuit. Before taking the bench, he practiced bankruptcy and business law for ten years in Los Angeles, and was a law professor for fourteen. He is the author or co-author of numerous articles, and of casebooks on contracts, bankruptcy, and commercial law. He is a conferee of the National Bankruptcy Conference, a fellow of the American College of Bankruptcy, a member of the International Insolvency Institute, and a member of the American Law Institute. He is the humorless co-author.

Lawrence Ponoroff is Dean of the James E. Rogers College of Law at the University of Arizona, where he also holds the Samuel M. Fegtly Chair in Commercial Law. Prior to that he was Dean and Mitchell Franklin Professor of Law at Tulane University Law School in New Orleans. A couple light years prior to that, he was a partner in the Denver-Colorado based law firm of Holme Roberts & Owen (now Bryan Cave HRO). Dean Ponoroff has received outstanding teaching awards at three different law schools. He is a Fellow of the American College of Bankruptcy as well as a member of the American Law Institute. He is also much nicer than his two co-authors, and almost as funny as Epstein.

Table of Contents

A SHORT AND HAPPY GUIDE TO CONTRACTS

Chapter 1

HAS A DEAL BEEN MADE? (OFFER AND ACCEPTANCE)

A. DETERMINING MUTUAL ASSENT

How do we know when and if the parties have reached "agreement" (mutual assent) on the terms of a deal as opposed to when they are still just negotiating over those terms? In the Anglo-American system of contract law, mutual assent is determined under *objective theory*. The inquiry, then, is what would a reasonable person in the position of each party believe based on the other party's words and conduct, regardless of what each party may have actually (subjectively) intended? Typically, but not always, mutual assent occurs in the form of an offer and an acceptance.

So, Epstein says to Ponoroff, "I will sell you my armadillo, named Armie, for $100." Ponoroff replies, "Sure, I'll give you $100 for Armie." If both Epstein and Ponoroff are reasonable in believing that the other means what he says, and neither has reason to know the other is not serious, then mutual assent has been achieved. It does not matter whether either or both of them really wanted, respectively, to buy or to sell Armie; the only thing that matters is that Epstein and Ponoroff both *outwardly manifested* a desire to buy or sell Armie.

Note that *both* prongs of objective theory must be satisfied. That is to say, a reasonable person in the position of the promisee must believe the other party intended to be bound *and* the promisee must have *actually so believed*. Thus, if Epstein says to Ponoroff, "I'll sell Armie to you for $100," but Ponoroff knows Epstein would not part with Armie for any price, then Ponoroff's assent to the

1

transaction will not create a contract, *even if* a reasonable person would have believed Epstein was dead serious.

It is not necessary, however, that either party expressly states an intent that his or her promise has legal consequences; that is presumed, although this presumption is usually not applied in promises involving purely social activities. So, if Ponoroff accepts Epstein's offer to sell Armie for $100, an enforceable contract is formed. This resembles a typical commercial transaction, and it is reasonable to believe that both parties intended to be bound. But if Ponoroff accepts Epstein's promise to take him to a Richmond Braves baseball game, an enforceable contract has perhaps not been formed, unless Epstein made clear in the offer that he intended to undertake a legally binding obligation in making the proposal. Similarly, should Epstein say, "I offer to sell you my armadillo for $100, but I do not intend this to be a legally binding obligation," then there is no mutual assent even if Ponoroff accepts. Why not? Think about objective theory. How could Ponoroff reasonably believe that Epstein intended to be bound by the offer when Epstein expressly said he did not?

The fact that the parties contemplate later reducing their agreement to writing also does not prevent them from being bound before the writing is signed if it is clear they intended the writing merely to serve as a formal memorial of their prior agreement. On the other hand, if it is understood between the parties that no obligation shall exist *until* the agreement has been reduced to a signed writing, then neither party is obligated to the other until that writing is signed. This rule can be found in § 27 of the *Restatement (Second) of Contracts*.

B.   OFFER

1.   In General

An offer is a promise by one party, made to another party, to do or not do something in the future, contingent upon the other party's acceptance. As is the case in connection with most contract formation issues, objective theory is applied when determining whether a particular communication—whether in the form of words, conduct, or some combination of each, constitutes an offer. If so, the offer creates in the offeree the "power of acceptance"; i.e., the ability to create a binding agreement with that party's assent alone.

Remember that an offer must (either directly or indirectly):

• Be communicated.

- Indicate a desire to enter into a contract.

- Be directed at some person or persons.

- Invite acceptance.

- Create a reasonable understanding that upon acceptance a contract will arise.

Epstein's promise to sell Armie the armadillo for $100 is a simple example of an offer. The tricky part is to understand *why* it's an offer. It is not because Epstein actually intends to offer Armie for sale, but because a reasonable person in Ponoroff's position would believe, based on the language used and all of the surrounding circumstances, that Epstein intends to be bound. Thus, contract formation occurs not upon an actual "meeting of the minds," but rather an apparent "meeting of the minds." Again, however, if Ponoroff knows or has reason to know that Epstein is not serious—through personal knowledge or inference from other circumstances, etc.—then Ponoroff does not have the power of acceptance because there is no offer.

2. Uncertainty About Offers: Price Quotes and Public Advertisements

Two types of communications that frequently create uncertainty with respect to whether an offer has been made are: (1) price quotes, and (2) general public advertisements. As a *general rule,* neither is an offer. Why not? Well, assume Markell's Grocery quotes a price of 10 cents per pound for melons or places an ad to that effect in the local newspaper. What should you, a reasonable person, infer in either case? Because merchants need some freedom to deliver information about their goods to the market without committing to anyone and everyone who raises her hand and says, "I accept," the logical answer is that the most reasonable inference is that Markell is inviting offers, not making one. Instead of giving the promisee(s) the power of acceptance, Markell is reserving the right of final assent before a deal arises.

But now suppose Epstein puts up a poster stating, "$50 reward for anyone who finds and returns my pet armadillo, Armie." If you return Armie, can you claim the reward? Sure you can. So what's different? First, only one person can return Armie. That means that there is no risk of obligation in excess of supply, unlike the melon advertisement. So, it is more reasonable in this case to infer that Epstein intends to pay whoever returns Armie. It is also more reasonable than in the typical general advertisement case to infer that Epstein is bargaining for the act of having Armie returned, and not that he is seeking offers from people to volunteer to go out looking for Armie. What's important is that it all comes down to the specific facts and circumstances of any situation and what it is reasonable for the recipient of the price quote or advertisement to infer in relation to the intent of the person making the quote or placing the ad. Put more directly, it all comes down to objective theory. The general rules exist because they are most often true, but that does *not* mean they are always true.

This might leave you just a bit frustrated. In fact, right now you may be muttering to yourself, "Why can't they just tell me *the answer*?" But in contract law, as in many areas of the law, the answer is "it depends," and it depends on what result best serves the purpose for the rule in the first place. The laws of society are not like the laws of physics; they are not about a fixed, immutable set of rules or principles. They are about achieving fair and efficient results. Don't despair, though. Think about it; if determining the answer to legal problems were always simple, there wouldn't be nearly as much need for lawyers, meaning you would make less money. Seriously, the lawyer's skill is not just to *know* the rules, but to know how skillfully to *apply* the rules. So celebrate and embrace ambiguity—or at least get used to it.

C. TERMINATION OF OFFER

Because we know you like to number things, we know you're going to be happy to learn that there are four ways in which an offer can be terminated.

i. Rejection

ii. Revocation

iii. Lapse

iv. Death (or incapacity) of the offeror (or the offeree)

Let's take them in turn.

1. Rejection

A rejection (as Epstein remembers well from his single days) occurs when the offeree declines the offer. It's that simple. And once the offer is terminated by rejection, it cannot be revived, no way and no how, *unless* the offeror chooses to revive it.

So, assume now that Ponoroff bought Epstein's armadillo, Armie, and the next day Epstein tells Ponoroff, "I'll also sell you

Armie's cage for $25." If Ponoroff says, "No, thanks," that's it; the offer has been expressly rejected and it's dead with no hope of resurrection. Likewise, the offer is also dead if Ponoroff says, "I'll give you $20 for the cage"; this is an *implied* rejection, but the effect is the same. The only difference between the express and implied rejection is that the latter creates a new offer (counteroffer) which the original offeror—in our case Epstein—can accept or not, as he chooses.

Rejection is absolute. Once Ponoroff has rejected the offer, he can no longer say, "No, wait, I accept." Likewise, even if Ponoroff gets desperate and offers $50 for Armie's cage after initially rejecting Epstein's offer, it's just too late. Ponoroff no longer has the power of acceptance once he rejects. He can only make new offers and hope Epstein accepts; but there is no longer anything for him to accept.

2. Revocation (the Offeror of Common Law Contracts; Namely, Is King)

Derived from the first principle of freedom of contract, an offeror retains complete mastery and control over her offer until acceptance. In a word, the offeror is "king," and thus may modify the terms of the offer at any time; he can also withdraw, or *revoke*, the offer any time he chooses. Once Epstein offers to sell Armie for $100 to Ponoroff, until Ponoroff accepts, Epstein can change any of the terms of the offer, or he can tell Ponoroff that he has changed his mind and is revoking the offer. And once revoked, the offer is dead—just as if it had been rejected—and Ponoroff can no longer accept, precisely because the revocation has stripped him of the power of acceptance.

Perhaps the only tricky aspect of revocation is the concept of an "indirect revocation," first illustrated in the 1876 English case of *Dickinson v. Dodds,* which is probably in your casebook. In the typical revocation scenario, the offeror withdraws (kills) her offer by notifying the offeree of her revocation. An indirect revocation occurs when the offeree learns from someone *other than* the offeror that the offeror is no longer interested in the deal.

For example, Epstein sends a letter offering to sell his armadillo, Armie, to Markell for $100. The next day, before Markell has responded, he runs into Ponoroff, one of Epstein's close confidants (despite the considerable difference in their ages). Markell tells Ponoroff about the offer and of his excitement at the prospect of acquiring Armie. Ponoroff replies, "Armie, the armadillo? You can't be serious. Epstein sold Armie to Robbie's Roadkill Restaurant last night." Devastated, Markell grabs a phone, calls Epstein and says,

"I accept your offer to buy Armie." Epstein replies, "Sorry, I've changed my mind." Can Markell successfully sue Epstein for breach of contract?

The answer is probably not, and the theory is that once Markell learned from an apparently reliable source—Ponoroff that Epstein was no longer of a mind to sell Armie to him, then the offer terminated no differently than if Epstein had communicated this information to Markell directly. Why? Objective theory, of course. That is, after his conversation with Ponoroff—and before he accepted—a reasonable person in Markell's position would no longer believe that Epstein still wanted to sell Armie to him. Markell doesn't need to hear directly from Epstein to learn that he no longer possesses the power of acceptance; it is sufficient that a reliable source relays the message because it achieves the same result.

Does it matter whether or not Epstein had really sold Armie to Robbie's? No. Does it matter if Markell believes that Epstein still wants to sell Armie to him for $100? No. Neither of these facts matter because the focus is on what an objective, reasonable person in Markell's position believes in regard to Epstein's intent after the conversation with Ponoroff. Thus, Markell's attempted acceptance simply becomes a new offer that Epstein may accept or, as in our example, not accept if he has changed his mind for any reason.

We realize that this concept of indirect revocation is a little difficult to wrap your mind around at first. But, in fact, it is perfectly consistent with the objective theory of contract formation and once you are able to articulate why that is so, you will be in a position to amaze friends and members of the opposite sex at parties?

Now, just to make sure you really have it here, let's assume the same facts except (1) Markell never speaks with Ponoroff, and (2) unbeknownst to Markell when he calls Epstein, in fact Epstein had entered into a contract to sell Armie to Robbie's. Is there a contract between Epstein and Markell? You bet. Is there also a contract between Epstein and Robbie's? Sure. Are they both enforceable? Yes. You mean, one party can enter into more than one contract for a single subject matter? Absolutely, but we don't recommend it, since Epstein necessarily will only be able to perform one contract and, thus, will unavoidably be in breach on the other. To be clear, the difference in this set of facts is that revocation was never *communicated* to Markell, directly or indirectly, so Epstein's offer was never revoked.

3. Lapse

Unlike the Highlander, no offer lives forever. Rather, **an offer lasts as long as the offeror says it will last for—assuming it is not earlier terminated by rejection or revocation.** But if the offer is for an unstated or indefinite period of time, we need a rule to tell us for how long it will remain open. Fortunately we have one. The rule is that an offer for an unstated period remains open for a—|drum roll|—*reasonable* time.

What constitutes a reasonable time will depend on all of the facts and circumstances, including market conditions and any prior course of dealing between the parties. As a general rule, however, when the offer is communicated in a face to face conversation, the offer lapses when the parties are, so to speak, no longer in one another's face. Of course, since the offeror is king, this general rule can be overcome by an expression of contrary intention in the offer. Indeed, the terms of the offer almost always control and should be consulted first. So, in the last example, one way Epstein could have avoided becoming liable under two separate contracts for the same armadillo would have been to specify in his offer to Markell that the offer would terminate automatically if Armie became subject to a prior contract for sale.

4. Death (or Incapacity) of the Offeror (or Offeree)

One of the more controversial rules of contract formation is that if the offeror dies (or is adjudicated incompetent) then the offer terminates automatically and without regard to whether the offeree was notified or aware of the death (or incapacity). Is this consistent with objective theory? Sadly, no; it is a glaring exception. But why? Well, it probably traces back to the oft-quoted adage that forming a contract involves a "meeting of the minds," and how can that occur when one mind has either shut down or gone out of its mind? In point of fact, however, the meeting of the minds required for contract formation under objective theory is, as we know, an *apparent*, not an *actual*, meeting of the minds. Thus, a minority view holds that death or incapacity does not terminate the offer until the offeree is aware of it, as with revocation and rejection.

Later, we will discuss what constitutes mental competence for purposes of capacity to contract. However, the rule of automatic termination when the offeror is determined to be incapacitated is even more vexing than the rule of automatic termination on death. Consider this situation: Epstein offers to sell his pet armadillo,

Armie, to Ponoroff for $100, and the offer provides it will remain open for two weeks. Ponoroff is interested, but won't commit until he has checked tuition and availability to sign Armie up for a six-week course at the Armadillo Obedience School. Knowing both that Epstein is *really* old and that the offer automatically terminates upon a party's death, Ponoroff can arguably protect himself and his armadillo-education down payments by calling Epstein every morning and making sure Epstein answers the phone. Life and death are fairly binary. But how much confidence can Ponoroff have that just because Epstein answers the phone Epstein still has all his marbles? Is it enough if each morning he inquires during the call, "Dave, you still playing with a full deck?" Even if Epstein says "yes," how much comfort does that really bring?

Note: The rule on automatic termination does not apply *after* acceptance. In that case, the only issue is whether there might be a defense based on the impossibility of performance—a subject we take up in Chapter 5. For now, understand that if Markell borrows $100 from Ponoroff, dying does not get him off the hook as far as the debt is concerned.

Finally, this rule applies not only to the death or incapacity of the offeror, but also to the offeree. In that scenario, however, the logic is that if the person with the power of acceptance is either dead or lacks capacity to accept because of mental incompetence, then there is no point in the offer continuing. This reasoning ignores, however, the fact that in many contexts the offer might still be valuable to the offeree's legal representative, who is unaware of what transpired. So it ought to make a difference—but under the majority rule does not—whether the offer was personal in nature (for the purchase and sale of opera tickets) or of economic value (for the sale of property at a favorable price that the executor of the estate might want to take advantage of on behalf of the heirs of the offeree).

D. PRESERVATION OF THE OFFER (OPTION CONTRACTS)

1. Traditional Option

Because the offeror retains complete mastery and control over her offer until acceptance, an offeree who wishes to take advantage of an offer should accept promptly. There are times, however, when the offeree is very interested in the offer (and wants to be sure it remains available to him), but is not yet prepared to assume liability under a contract by accepting. For example, suppose Epstein offers to sell Armie, the armadillo, to Markell for $100.

Markell would love to have Armie (it's a lifelong dream) but Markell doesn't have $100. So he needs to arrange financing. That's going to take some time, and there's no guaranty that his loan will be approved. Thus, he does not want to accept until he knows he has the money, but, in the meantime, he runs the risk that at any moment Epstein will withdraw the offer, die, or lose his mind. What can Markell do?

Well, Markell can ask Epstein to hold the offer open for the amount of time he needs to find out if his financing has been approved. Even if Epstein agrees, however, that won't get the job done because, recall, an offer for a stated period of time is good for the time stated, *unless* it's earlier terminated by revocation or the like. What does that mean? It means the promise to hold the offer open for X days, just like any other promise, is *not* enforceable unless it is itself part of an exchange transaction; i.e., supported by consideration. Therefore, in order to guard against revocation or other termination of the offer until such time has sorted out his financing, Markell will have to offer Epstein consideration. In other words, Epstein needs to receive something in return for his promise to keep the offer to Markell open, separate and apart from what he stands to gain ($100) under the principal contract. [If you are a little confused by this "consideration" concept, worry not, as we will explain it in the next chapter.]

How does this work? Terminology can get a little tricky here. Let's suppose Markell says to Epstein: "In return for $1, will you hold your offer to sell Armie to me open for one week"? If Epstein says "yes," an *option contract* has been formed. That is, Markell now has the choice for one week to accept or not accept Epstein's offer without having to fear a revocation. Sometimes in these circumstances, however, instead of referring to a separate option contract, Epstein's offer to sell Armie simply will be described as an *irrevocable offer*. The effect is the same: for one week, Markell is protected against withdrawal of the offer and, in return, Epstein has a dollar he would not otherwise have.

2. UCC "Option"

While the exchange of consideration represents the traditional mechanism for making an offer irrevocable, there are other means by which the same result might attain in contemporary contract law doctrine. For instance, under § 2–205 of Article 2, an offer: (a) made by a person in the business of selling goods of that kind (i.e., a "merchant"), (b) in writing, (c) that provides that it will be held open, may not be revoked, even without consideration, for the period stated, or if no period is stated, for a period not to exceed three months. This is what's referred to as a "firm offer." The theory is that a merchant who makes such a promise knows the score, and the presence of a signed writing serves to assure that the promise to hold the offer open was a deliberative one.

3   Reliance as a Basis to Create an Option

Finally, under § 87(2) of the *Restatement (Second) of Contracts,* an offer that foreseeably induces detrimental reliance of a substantial character by the offeree may be enforced as a binding option contract, to the extent necessary to prevent injustice, despite the absence of both (1) a promise of irrevocability, and (2) consideration in support of that promise. In effect, this protects the offeree's reasonable reliance on the offer by implying a promise to hold the offer open, even when no such express promise has been made, and to enforce that promise, even though unsupported by consideration. So if Epstein offers to sell Armie, the armadillo, to Markell knowing that Markell plans to pay the large and non-refundable registration fee to enter Armie into Ponoroff's armadillo marathon, Epstein might be precluded for a reasonable time from withdrawing that offer, even though he neither promised to hold the offer open for a stated period nor received anything from Markell in return for holding it open.

So, by way of summary, remember the following:

- **All offers, standing alone, are revocable.**

- **Even offers that are stated to be irrevocable are revocable, unless:**

  - **The promise not to revoke is supported by consideration,**

  - **The promise is made enforceable by statute (i.e., the firm offer), or**

  - **The promise (whether or not said to be irrevocable) induces substantial reliance**

E. ACCEPTANCE (THE OTHER HALF OF THE MUTUAL ASSENT PUZZLE)

Generally speaking, an acceptance is a manifestation of assent, objectively determined, to be bound by the terms of the offer. It is the exercise of the power of acceptance (created by the offer) that simultaneously brings the agreement into existence and terminates the offeror's ability to revoke.

1. Three "Rules" About Acceptance

- **The offeree must have knowledge of the offer (intend to accept)**

- **Only the offeree can accept an offer**

- **The acceptance must be in the form authorized by the offer**

Let's consider each of these general rules about acceptances in turn:

a. Intent to Accept

Suppose Epstein posts a reward of $25 for anyone who finds and returns his lost armadillo, Armie. Ponoroff is unaware of the reward, but sees Armie trying to sneak into an adult entertainment club. Recognizing that it's Armie, he grabs the varmint and brings him back to Epstein. Later that day, he sees a flyer offering the reward and seeks to collect from Epstein. If Epstein says, "No way, dude," is Ponoroff out of luck? Probably so. By definition, an offeree can't manifest assent to an offer he doesn't even know about. On the other hand, since Epstein did get what he was bargaining for—return of Armie—why shouldn't he have to pay? Perhaps this is where one might make a *policy* argument.

The modern approach adopts the view that, if an offeree learns of the offer in the midst of the requested performance, the completion of performance is sufficient to constitute acceptance, since there is no point in requiring the offeree to start over again. That probably doesn't help Ponoroff in our example, but could make a difference where Ponoroff, two weeks after purchasing and using the Miracle–Gro Hair Restorer learns of an offer by the manufacturer to pay $10 to anyone who "uses our product for four weeks." If Ponoroff continues his use of the product for two additional weeks, he should be able to claim the $10.

b. Who May Accept

The power of acceptance is personal to the offeree. If Ponoroff offers to sell his armadillo to Markell, Epstein, who perhaps who long coveted that armadillo as a companion for Armie, cannot accept. Why not? Because Epstein lacks the power of acceptance. This is totally consistent with both objective theory and the notion that the offeror is master of her offer. That is to say, Epstein would not be reasonable in believing that his assent to an offer made to Markell would create a binding contract between him and

Ponoroff. Likewise, contract liability is volitional; Ponoroff cannot be forced into a contract with someone to whom he made no offer.

c.   Manner of Acceptance

Once more, because the offeror is king and may stipulate the terms on which he is prepared to deal (and is bound on none others without his consent), the traditional rule is that an acceptance, to be effective, must conform to any and all requirements specified in the offer. That means if an offer stipulates the time, place, and or manner of acceptance, to be effective, an effort to accept must comply with that stipulation without variation. So, assume Epstein says to Markell, "I offer to sell Armie to you for $100, and you may signify your acceptance by placing a paper bag over your head and, while dancing in a circle, squawk like a chicken." If Markell responds by simply saying "I accept," no contract is formed because Markell did not comply with the form of acceptance stipulated in the offer.

At its core, this rule has its origins in the notion that the offeror is king, and, therefore, should not be forced to deal on terms other than those she has specified. But sometimes the offeror may have specified the time, place, and/or manner of acceptance merely as a convenience; not because she really cared. In those situations, under the traditional rule, a non-complying acceptance will not give rise to a contract even in circumstances where that result may frustrate the desire and intent of the offeror. Thus, the *Restatement (Second)*, §§ 30(2) & 32, softens the classical contract law approach by providing that, unless otherwise indicated, an offer will be treated as inviting acceptance in any manner reasonable in the circumstance, including return promise or performance of what is requested by the offer. The UCC is in accord. *See* § 2–206. Under the contemporary standard, then, a specified manner of acceptance is regarded as a mere convenience, that does not preclude acceptance in any other reasonable manner, *unless* the offer *clearly and unambiguously* indicates that the designated manner of assent is exclusive (after all, the offeror is still king).

2.   Communication and Effectiveness of Acceptance

a.   General Rules

Under classical contract law principles, every offer had to be characterized as either unilateral or bilateral; that is, as seeking acceptance by, respectively, either an act (unilateral) or a return promise (bilateral), and an acceptance was

proper only if it complied accordingly. Therefore, if Markell offered Ponoroff $20 to "wash and wax my car," the only way for Ponoroff to accept would have been to do the work. Correspondingly, if Markell said, "I'll pay you $20 if you agree to wash and wax my car," Ponoroff would need to promise to do so ("I agree") in order to create a binding contract. By definition, a unilateral contract is executory only on one side (because the other party performed as part of her acceptance), and a bilateral contract is, at the moment of formation, wholly executory.

The rigid distinction between offers for unilateral and bilateral contracts found in older cases was fairly artificial and, when strictly applied, could produce results that conflicted with the real intent of the parties. For example, Markell might phrase his offer, "I'll pay you $20 to wash and wax my car," which would likely be construed as an offer for a performance. But does Markell really care, or even think about, the desired form of acceptance? If Ponoroff agrees, why should either party be able to walk from the deal because a promissory acceptance is not a permissible way to accept an offer for a unilateral contract? **Therefore, as we have seen, the contemporary view is that regardless of how the offer is framed, it may be accepted by any reasonable manner of assent, unless the offer leaves *no doubt* that it can only be accepted in the manner stipulated in the offer.** So, in the example above, "I'll pay you $20 to wash and wax my car," Ponoroff might accept either by doing the job or responding, "I accept."

Consistent with objective theory, acceptance of an offer by return promise is not effective of course until *communicated* to the offeror, although an exception applies if the offeror has dispensed with that requirement. If not, until the acceptance is communicated, the offeror remains king; i.e., may withdraw the offer. This can be important when the parties are at a distance from one another and there will be a gap between the time an acceptance is made (a written offer is accepted by signing) and the time it is actually communicated to the offeror (the signed offer is returned). The logic here is that a non-communicated promise is antithetical to the very notion of making a promise. The rule, however, is different when acceptance is by performance because the offer is construed as permitting or requiring acceptance in that fashion. In these instances, courts take the position that notice is not necessary based on the fact that the offeror is bargaining for the act to be done, so that the completion of the act alone is enough to bind the offeror without further notice.

b. The "Mailbox Rule"

The so-called Mailbox Rule is a rule that is becoming increasingly unimportant as a practical matter, but one that Contracts professors love to test, so we better talk about it. Established by the famous English case of *Adams v. Lindsell,* the mailbox rule comes into play when there is a period of delay in the parties' communications, as might occur when the negotiations are being conducted, for example, through the use of mail.

The Mailbox rule holds that, unless the offer prescribes to the contrary, an acceptance sent by a reasonable means is effective on *dispatch* (and not receipt). Along with the rule on automatic termination of an offer on death, this is a glaring exception to the objective theory of contract formation. It also runs contrary to the rule that a promissory acceptance is not effective until communicated, at least to the extent "communicated" is understood as actually made known to the offeror.

The rationale for the Mailbox Rule (which is more appropriately dubbed the Dispatch Rule and which is how we'll refer to it from now on) first articulated in *Adams v. Lindsell* was that, since the offer was made by mail, the offeror had *impliedly* authorized acceptance in the same manner. This is fine as far as it goes, but it's a fairly weak justification for also concluding that the offeror also assented to be bound upon mailing rather than receipt.

There is a better rationale for the Dispatch Rule and, that is, it is needed to allocate the risk of transmission. In other words, when an acceptance is sent, for example, by mail, it could get lost or delayed on its journey. Who should bear that risk? There's something to be said in making that choice to allocate the risk to the party who had the power to control the risk. That would be the offeror, who could have negated the Dispatch Rule by providing, for example, in the offer that an acceptance would only become effective if and when actually received. By contrast, the offeree has no way to protect herself from uncertainty during the period of transmission, including from the possibility of receiving the offeror's revocation *before* the offeree's acceptance arrives.

We think a few examples might help you to understand the operation of the Dispatch Rule in action: Assume the following:

- Day 1: Epstein sends Ponoroff a letter offering to sell Armie (the armadillo) for $100. The letter is silent as to manner of acceptance.

- Day 2: Epstein realizes he's far too attached to Armie to sell him, so he mails a revocation of his offer.

- Day 3: Ponoroff receives Epstein's offer and mails an acceptance.

- Day 5: Ponoroff receives Epstein's revocation.

- Day 6: Epstein receives Ponoroff's acceptance.

(1) Is there a contract between Epstein and Ponoroff?

Yes, formed on the mailing of the acceptance by Ponoroff on Day 3.

(2) Does it matter if Epstein dies on Day 3?

No, death terminates an offer, not a binding contract.

(3) Does it matter if Epstein dies on Day 2?

Maybe, depending if he died before or after Ponoroff dispatched his acceptance (creating some interesting proof issues).

(4) Does it matter if Ponoroff misaddresses his acceptance or fails to attach adequate postage?

Yes. Even if acceptance by return mail is authorized, the offeree will lose the benefit of the mailbox rule if he is careless in sending his reply, as in this example, or in a case where the letter is misaddressed.

(5) Would it change the analysis if Ponoroff first sent a rejection on Day 3 and then, later in the day, sent the acceptance (bearing in mind that rejections are not effective until receipt)?

Yes, under these circumstances, the Dispatch Rule is rendered ineffective and whether or not there is a contract will depend on which communication is received first. If the rejection arrives first, there is no contract. If the acceptance overtakes the rejection and arrives first, the contract is formed on receipt of the acceptance. See *Restatement (Second) of Contracts* § 40.

The Dispatch Rule also does not apply in the case of option contracts since the offeree is protected against an unexpected revocation during the option period. Thus, if Markell pays Ponoroff $1 for a 30–day option to purchase the Grand Canyon from Ponoroff for $100 and mails his notice of exercise of the option on day 29, it will only be effective *if received* by Ponoroff before the end of day 30. If it arrives on the 31st day, it's too late because the offer lapsed.

To summarize, the Dispatch Rule:

- Applies when there is a gap between dispatch and receipt of an acceptance

- Is only activated when the offeree uses the authorized means of communication (or a more reliable means)

- Applies only to acceptances (revocations, counteroffers, and rejections are effective upon receipt)

- Doesn't apply when an acceptance follows a rejection or counteroffer

- Doesn't apply if an offer is irrevocable (option contract)

- Doesn't apply when communication is near instantaneous (e-mail)

c.   The *Restatement (Second)* and the Effectiveness of Acceptance

Section 63 of the *Restatement (Second) of Contracts* continues to recognize the Dispatch Rule with respect to promissory acceptances sent in a manner authorized by the offer. However, § 64 provides that an acceptance by telephone or other means of substantially instantaneous (think e-mail, texting, and Facebook) two-way communication is governed by the principles applicable when the parties are in the presence of one another, meaning that the offeror must actually be aware of the acceptance. In effect, when the gap between transmission and receipt is minimal, the rational for the Dispatch Rule—to allocate the risk of transmission—is no longer operative. Recall our mentioning that the Dispatch Rule is becoming less important. In an era where commerce is increasingly occurring through interaction of electronic agents, this exception has rendered the Dispatch Rule far less important that it was even 20 years ago.

The *Restatement (Second)* also continues the traditional rule that an acceptance by performance is effective without the need of notification to the offeror (unless the offer *requires* notification). The *Restatement (Second)*, however, adds a twist to this rule. Specifically, § 54(2) provides that the offeror's duty to perform is discharged if the offeree who has rendered performance fails to take reasonable steps to ensure that the offeror learns of the performance. Thus, suppose Markell leaves for an extended vacation in Paducah after offering Ponoroff $20 to wash and wax Markell's car. A contract binding Markell arises as soon as Ponoroff completes the job, but if Ponoroff is not reasonably diligent in making sure Markell is aware that the work has been done; Markell's duty to pay may be discharged.

In addition to acceptance by promise or performance, § 62 of the *Restatement (Second)* treats partial performance as a form of promissory acceptance, so long as that possibility is not precluded expressly by the terms of the offer. Hence, when Markell offers Ponoroff $20 to wash and wax his car and Ponoroff commences performance, a contract is formed under which both parties are bound—Ponoroff to complete the job and Markell to pay. Finally, if the offer does clearly and unambiguously preclude acceptance by any means other than full performance—Markell, as he has the right to do, makes clear that he was bargaining for Ponoroff's performance and nothing less will do—then the commencement of that performance creates an *option* in Ponoroff's favor to give him a reasonable amount of time to finish the job. Obviously, this rule, set forth in *Restatement (Second)* § 45, is intended to protect Ponoroff from a revocation by Markell after he puts in a lot of work on the job; i.e., has relied on the offer to his detriment.

3. Imperfect Acceptances (and Counteroffers)

Under the traditional of "Mirror Image Rule," an acceptance had to be an unconditional expression of assent to the terms of the offer without addition or variation—anything less than that would be regarded as a counteroffer—thereby placing the power of acceptance back in the hands of the original offeror. The justification for this rule was that an offeror should not be bound to any terms other than those to which she had expressed a willingness to deal. The mirror-image rule parallels the classical contract law approach regarding *manner* of acceptance when stated in the offer, except here the focus is on the *content* of the acceptance.

Strictly applied, the mirror-image rule (just like the traditional rule on manner of acceptance) can work some rather harsh and unexpectedly restrictive results in terms of protecting the interests of the offeror and enforcing arrangements to which, in point of fact, the parties really intended to be bound. For instance, on Friday, Epstein e-mails Ponoroff, "I'll sell my pet armadillo, Armie, to you for $100, exchange of money and reptile to take place in front of the law school on Tuesday." Ponoroff replies, "I accept, but it would be much more convenient for me if we could make the exchange on Wednesday." Epstein assumes he and Ponoroff have a deal. He really doesn't care whether the deal is consummated on Tuesday or

Wednesday, and figures he'll work that out with Ponoroff on Monday after he gets back from a weekend at his summer place on the Cape. On Sunday, Ponoroff sends Epstein an e-mail saying, "I've changed my mind; I don't even like Armie, so no deal." Can Epstein recover if he sues? Under the classical common law analysis, the answer would be "no," because Ponoroff's reply was a counteroffer that Epstein failed to accept before it was revoked by Ponoroff.

Recognizing that strict application of the mirror-image rule produced results at variance with actual intent, modern cases (and the *Restatement (Second)*) distinguish between an acceptance with "a suggestion or inquiry," as in our example, and a truly conditional acceptance; e.g., "I accept, provided that the exchange occurs on Wednesday, not Tuesday." Only the latter is an implied rejection and a counteroffer. In our example, a contract exists between Epstein and Ponoroff for the sale of Armie on Tuesday, with a request that Epstein consider delaying delivery and payment by a day. Not coincidentally, the evolution of the law in this area—from a bright-line rule to a more flexible standard—coincides with the evolution that we saw earlier in the rules governing the manner of acceptance.

In contracts involving the sale of goods, the drafters of the UCC took a somewhat different, and certainly far more complex, approach to this issue than the common law mirror image rule. If the response to an offer for the sale of goods adds or changes terms, you will need to look to § 2–207.

Here's one example of how § 2–207 works. Markell, a widget manufacturer, sends Epstein, a widget retailer, one of his pre-printed purchase order forms, which has been filled in to request 100 widgets at $50 per widget, delivery to take place at Markell's place of business on or before July 1. Epstein replies by sending one of his pre-printed acknowledgement forms back to Markell. With respect to all the negotiated terms of the transaction, such as price quantity, delivery terms, etc., the acknowledgement has been completed so that is identical to the purchase order. On the back of Epstein's form, however, there is some standard printed language providing that the goods are being sold without warranty of any kind. The widgets are shipped to Markell, who accepts and pays for them. Two months later, Markell discovers what he believes is a defect in the widgets, and so he brings a claim for breach of warranty.

Will Markell prevail? Under the mirror-image rule the answer would be "no," since the acceptance did not match the offer. Therefore, it would be treated as a counteroffer, which in turn would have been regarded as accepted by Markell's receipt of and payment for the goods. Thus, Markell has no warranty claim. It seems in this instance that the offeror, who was supposed to be the king, got royally screwed because Epstein had the "last shot" advantage. Let's see how 2–207 changes the result (brace yourself):

- **Step 1**—The Gateway: **Section 2–207(1) says that a definite and seasonable expression of assent shall constitute an acceptance even though it contains additional or different terms.** Because Epstein's acknowledgement matches Markell's purchase order on all of the specific deal points, it qualifies as an acceptance. By contrast, if the acknowledgement had indicated a price of $60 per widget, then we would *not* have a seasonable expression of assent, meaning that § 2–207(1) simply would not apply because we never got through the Gateway and the imperfect acceptance is just a counteroffer.

- **Step 2**—Conditional vs. Unconditional: **Even a definite and seasonable expression of assent won't get through the Gateway if the offeree makes explicit that her assent is *expressly* made contingent on the offeror's further assent to the additional or different terms contained in the acceptance.** So, if Epstein's acknowledgement said, "This acceptance is subject to and conditioned upon Markell's further assent to the additional terms herein contained," then, once more, you don't get past the Gateway. Most courts take the view that for an acceptance to be regarded as "expressly conditional," it is not enough to say the acceptance is "subject to the terms and conditions of this acknowledgement." Rather, the offeree must make clear its unwillingness to go forward without the other party's affirmative agreement to the additional or different terms. Epstein's acknowledgement was not so conditioned, so it qualifies as an acceptance under §2–207(1).

- **Step 3**—Additional Terms: Once the offeree's acceptance makes it through the Gateway of § 2–207(1), the next question becomes what do you do with the additional or different terms? **This brings us to § 2–207(2), which provides that additional terms are *proposals* that only become part of the contract upon the assent of the offeror.** There is an exception, however, when the contract is between two merchants. In that situation, the additional terms *will* become part of the contract, *unless*: (1) the offer expressly precludes additional terms, (2) the additional terms materially alter the offer, or (3) the offeror objects to them within a reasonable time. In our example, Markell and Epstein appear to be merchants; the offer does not expressly limit acceptance to the terms of the offer; and there is no indication that Markell objected to the disclaimer. That means the warranty disclosure is included in the contract unless it is deemed a material alteration: e.g. one that would result in surprise or hardship if incorporated into the contract without express awareness of the other party. While the concept of "materiality" is inherently vague, a warranty disclaimer would likely be found a sufficiently important change so as to be regarded a material alteration. Thus, the disclaimer is *not* part of the contract and Markell can proceed with his breach of warranty claim.

- **Step 4**—Agreement by Conduct: Next, suppose the acknowledgement from Epstein was expressly contingent on Markell's affirmative assent to the additional term. In that case, the documents would not form a contract. If Epstein nevertheless ships, and Markell nevertheless accepts and pays, surely there is some contract, but what are its terms? **This takes us to § 2–207(3), which essentially says that if a contract was not formed under § 2–207(1) & (2), but the parties conduct nevertheless demonstrates that some contract *does* exist, then the terms of that contract consist of the terms on which the two writings agree and such other terms as are supplied by default under Article 2.** In this case, the writings do not agree about a warranty. However, there is a provision of Article 2—§ 2–714(1)—that says a warranty that goods are free from defects is implied in every contract where the seller is a merchant, *unless* disclaimed. Our contract does not contain a disclaimer, and so Markell's claim for breach of warranty can go forward.

- **Step back**—Different Terms: In our original example, the "acceptance" contained an *additional* terms. Section 2–207(1) also applies to different terms. Re-read the first bold sentence of "Step 1" above. Section 2–207(2) however, is silent about the treatment of different terms. Suppose Markell's purchase order had provided for a one-year warranty; whereas the acknowledgement from Epstein stipulated that the widgets would be accompanied by a 90–day warranty to the exclusion of any other warranty. If, after six months, a defect shows up in the widgets, are the goods still under warranty? **Courts have taken three approaches to the question of what are the terms of the contract based on a response to an offer containing different terms.**

- The first approach is to treat different terms just like additional terms for purposes of § 2–207(2). Under this approach, Epstein's limitation of the warranty would only apply if the court were to find that it did not materially alter the agreement.

- The second approach, known as "fall-out," holds that the conflicting term in the offeree's acceptance simply drops out. In our case, this means that the one-year warranty provision would apply.

- The third approach, and the one representing the majority of reported decisions, takes the view that the conflicting terms knock each other out—neither becomes part of the contract. This leaves the parties with the remaining terms and the default provisions supplied by Article 2. As we saw earlier, there is an implied warranty in Article 2, which lasts a *reasonable* time. So, whether or not there is a claim would depend on whether six months exceeded a reasonable time.

- **Two-step**—Delayed Terms: There is some disagreement over whether § 2–207 applies to delayed terms in the case of so-called "rolling contracts." The typical example of a rolling contract arises when a consumer orders a product, such as a computer, online or by phone, and pays with a credit card. Usually, there is a right for a limited number of days after the computer arrives to return it for a full refund. When the computer arrives at the buyer's home and is opened, inevitably there is a packet of "Standard Terms & Conditions" enclosed in the box. Whether these Standard Terms provisions—including perhaps one providing for arbitration of disputes—are analyzed under § 2–207 depends on when the court concludes the contract was formed. If the contract was formed when the order was placed or the computer delivered, then the answer would be "yes." If, on the other hand, the contract is regarded as not formed until the right of return period expires without the buyer returning the system, then the answer is "no." Note that there are other cases that, while finding that the delayed terms are part of the contract without regard to § 2–207, have nevertheless refused to enforce the some of these provisions as *unconscionable*. We will address the subject of unconscionability in Chapter 3. For now regard it as meaning *way* unfair.

- **Watch your step**—Confirmations: Although § 2–207 is known as the "battle of the forms" provision, in fact, it is much broader and not limited to cases where there are two forms. Section 2–207(1), for example, refers—in addition to a definite and seasonable expression of acceptance—to confirmatory memoranda sent within a reasonable time. Thus, if Markell and Epstein reach an oral agreement over the phone for the purchase and sale of Armie, and Epstein thereafter sends a written confirmation of the deal to Markell that contains additional or different terms, § 2–207 determines whether those different or additional terms become part of the deal.

The diagram that follows may help you better see how § 2–207 operates—or it may just give you a headache. Bear in mind that the "imperfect acceptance" in subsection (1)—the definite and seasonable expression of acceptance—only qualifies as an acceptance if (a) it does not diverge in any significant way from the terms of the offer that are specific to the particular transaction at issue; i.e., price, quantity, delivery requirements, description of the goods, and (b) it is not affirmatively made conditional on the offeror's further assent to the additional or different terms.

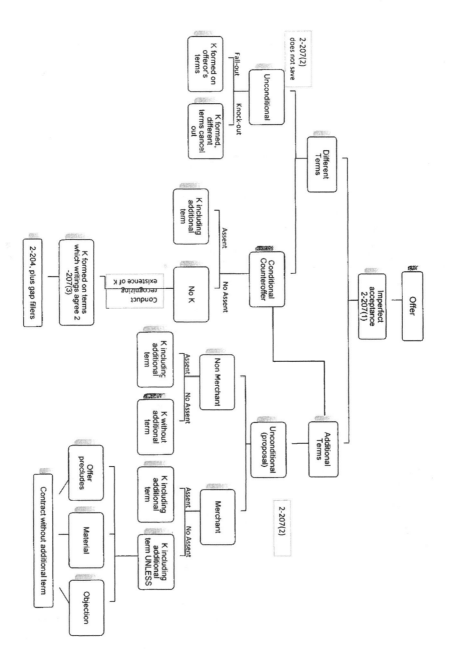

4.   Acceptance by Silence (or Inaction)

As a general rule, silence cannot constitute an acceptance. This is because silence alone is inherently ambiguous so the offeror is not reasonable in inferring much of anything from it. There is also the potential for an unscrupulous seller to foist unwanted goods on unsuspecting buyers. For example, suppose Epstein sends Markell a letter offering to sell to Markell Epstein's armadillo, Armie, for $1,000,000. The letter further states, "if I don't hear from you within seven days to the contrary, then we have a deal." When the letter arrives, Markell notices from the return address that it's from Epstein, so, of course, he throws it away. Would it be fair to regard Markell as having agreed, one week later, to pay $1,000,000 for Armie? Of course not.

On the other hand, there are some circumstances where an acceptance may be implied from the offeree's silence, or, put more precisely, where the silence is coupled with conduct that makes the inference of assent reasonable. **Silence in the face of receipt and enjoyment of a benefit with knowledge of an expectation of payment creates a contract.** Consider the situation where, to supplement his meager law professor income, Ponoroff operates a hot dog vending cart on 5th Avenue in Manhattan. There is a large sign on the cart displaying the price for the various dogs that Ponoroff has available for sale. Markell, who is in New York to experience new cuisine, happens past Ponoroff's stand; he points to a polish sausage and, upon being handed it by Ponoroff, consumes it on the spot. When Ponoroff requests payment, Markell argues that he never promised to pay [he also inquires of Ponoroff, "Do you know who I am"?]. As usual, we think Markell loses, because an implied-in-fact (implied from conduct) contract was formed when Markell accepted and enjoyed the sausage.

Silence (or acquiescence) when construed against a prior course of dealing might also constitute acceptance. Thus, in the example above, assume there was no price sign on the cart and Markell did not realize Ponoroff expected to be paid for his wieners. The first time Markell eats the sausage he might not be liable for its price. But, if on five previous occasions, every time Markell received and consumed a polish sausage from Ponoroff's cart he paid for it, this course of dealing could be regarded as giving sufficient meaning to the conduct that Markell could not escape paying for the next one.

Both of the instances described above where silence might be regarded as an acceptance are intended to protect the offeror from a sneaky offeree. Sometimes, though, it's the offeree who needs protection from the general rule that silence is not an acceptance. This might occur where the offeror tells the offeree that silence or acquiescence will be regarded as acceptance. If, in reliance on that assurance, the offeree, intending to accept, remains silent, the offeror who induced the reliance may not escape liability.

F. MUTUAL MISUNDERSTANDING OF CONTRACT TERMS

The doctrine of mutual misunderstanding applies when the parties agree to the use of the same term, but each attaches a different meaning to that term. These cases are to be distinguished from the doctrine of mistake (which we take up in Chapter 3), under which the parties may be excused from performing an agreement that was entered into based on a belief shared by both parties that ultimately proved not in accord with the facts.

Let's say that Epstein actually owns two armadillos named Armie (we know it's bizarre, but at Epstein's advanced age with failing eyesight and memory, he thinks all armadillos look like former U.S. House majority leader, Dick Armey). One of the armadillos is a prized runner, and Ponoroff is dying to get his hands-on him, so he offers Epstein $100 to purchase Armie. Epstein quickly accepts because he thinks Ponoroff is offering to buy Armie, the troublesome varmint, not Armie, the prized runner. When Ponoroff comes to pick up Armie, he is shocked to see the mischievous armadillo that he retrieved from the adult entertainment club. This would be a case of misunderstanding. On the other hand, if both parties meant the same Armie, but it turns out that, unbeknownst to either of them, Armie was a sloth and not really an armadillo, then we would have a mutual mistake case.

The case you doubtless read, or will read, in class about mutual misunderstanding is *Raffles v. Wichelhaus,* the English case involving the sale of cotton to be transported from Bombay to London on the ship *Peerless,* except it turned out, improbably, that there were two ships by that name on the same route sailing two months apart. The court, accepting the buyer's testimony that it had intended the *Peerless* sailing in October, rather than the one on which the cotton was actually shipped in December, concluded that the buyer's refusal to accept and pay for the cotton when tendered was not a breach since there had been no mutual assent.

Raffles has been subjected to a lot of criticism, including over the fact that it did not appear that the buyer protested when the seller failed to deliver the cotton after the earlier arrival of the October *Peerless.* There is also serious question as to whether the identity of the ship by which the cotton would be shipped was really an important term or just a way of assigning risk of loss should the ship go down. In other words, was this just a contract for the sale of cotton, or the contract for the sale of cotton on board a specific ship? Only in the latter case should the fact that there were two ships *Peerless* have made a difference.

Under the ***Restatement (Second) § 20,*** the doctrine of mutual misunderstanding has been more carefully refined to apply only in cases where a different meaning is attached to a material term and (1) neither party knows or has reason to know the meaning attached by the other, or (2) each party does know or have reason to know the meaning attached by the other. So, in our example, if *both* Ponoroff and Epstein share the erroneous belief about which Armie is actually for sale, and if this mistaken fact is *material* to the bargain— Epstein wouldn't have been willing to sell his esteemed runner for only $100, and Ponoroff wouldn't have been willing to spend $100 on Armie, the rabble-rouser—then the misunderstanding is mutual and the agreement will not be enforced. Things would come out quite differently, however, if Ponoroff knows Epstein means scoundrel Armie but does not clarify the point hoping to bring a claim for prized runner Armie. In this case, not only would the doctrine of mutual misunderstanding be inapplicable, but Ponoroff would be stuck with binding agreement for scoundrel Armie.

G. INDEFINITENESS AND DEFERRED AGREEMENT

Often the parties to an agreement will fail to express their agreement clearly, or, on occasions, will deliberately defer agreement on one or more of the key terms of the deal. We address each of these situations in turn.

1. Indefinite and Missing Terms

It is neither practicable nor realistic to expect that the parties to a deal will express every point of their agreement with perfect clarity. If a dispute breaks out between the parties, how is the court to enforce the deal if some of its terms are unclear or omitted? In answering that question, the court must balance the traditional understanding of contract liability as being about effectuating the private intent of the parties against the competing policy that clear contractual intent, once reached, not be thwarted.

The governing standard is generally expressed along the following lines. **If either: (a) the terms of the contract are so indefinite that it would be difficult or impossible for the court to detect a breach, or (b) even if a breach could be detected, but it is difficult or impossible for the court to fashion a remedy, then the contract is "too indefinite" to enforce. In other words, some vagueness will be tolerated, but "way vague" is too much.**

Older cases took a somewhat rigid approach to indefiniteness, meaning that in situations falling within either of the above circumstances the court simply would not enforce the agreement. Thus, if Ponoroff agreed to wash and wax Markell's car, but the agreement specified neither the time performance was to take place nor the amount Ponoroff was to be paid for his services, the agreement would fail under the traditional standard, despite the fact that both Markell and Ponoroff thought they had a deal and intended to be bound.

Both the *Restatement (Second)* and the UCC exhibit a much higher tolerance for indefiniteness and adopt a much more flexible approach to the problem designed to preserve contractual intent once it is found to exist. **Generally speaking, the indefiniteness analysis occurs in two steps: (1) whether the parties intended to enter into a legally binding deal, and, if so, (2) whether there is a reasonably certain basis for the court to fashion an appropriate remedy**. The more indefinite the agreement, the more likely it is that the parties did not intend to be bound.

The principal difference, however, between the traditional and modern approaches is the willingness of courts today to imply missing or unclear terms. Thus, if Ponoroff and Markell fail to specify the time for Ponoroff's performance or the amount Markell must pay, a court today, that found that both parties intended to be bound, might still enforce the deal, concluding that performance must occur within a reasonable time and the price would be the going market rate for comparable services.

In sale of goods contracts, the UCC incorporates a number of so-called "gap fillers" like these that apply *unless* the parties provide otherwise. In essence, they operate as "default rules" that apply whenever the agreement is silent as to the subject of one of the gap-fillers. The major policy question to be considered when a court supplies a missing term to the deal, assuming there is a reasonable basis for doing so, is whether this refers to a reasonable basis for assuming that the parties *intended* that the court would provide the missing or ambiguous term, or just an objectively reasonable basis for supplying or construing the missing or vague term. In other words, is the court just effectuating the intent of the parties (the traditional role of courts in contract cases) or is the court actually kind of making-up some parts of the deal using objectively "fair" terms?

2. Deferred Agreement

"Agreements to agree" present a different kind of indefiniteness issue. In these cases, there is no question that the parties have yet to reach agreement on some aspect of their deal; such as, rent during a lease renewal term, or the price to be paid for goods in years two and three of a three-year contract. Therefore, traditionally, these arrangements were treated as completely unenforceable if the parties failed to later reach actual agreement as to a material term.

The realities of modern commercial transactions, however, suggest that agreements to agree can serve useful and important commercial purposes. Not uncommonly today, instead of "one-shot" transactions involving short, impersonal dealings, many business deals will involve long-term, complex arrangements. In these cases where performance may span several years, perhaps neither party wants to accept the risk of setting a price today for goods and services that will be rendered far into the future. In these circumstances it makes sense for them to say, "We will set the price at the time when prevailing market conditions are known." When everything goes according to plan, the parties will later come to an agreement on the open term, and everyone is happy. If the parties fail to come to an agreement, the court will have to decide whether the agreement is too indefinite to enforce or whether the court can save the deal by supplying the missing terms.

H.   PRECONTRACTUAL LIABILITY

Generally, the parties cannot become obligated to one another *before* mutual assent; i.e., before they have reached a deal. Contract liability is voluntary or consensual, so until the parties have actually *agreed* to be bound to the terms of the deal, either party may walk away from the negotiations without liability. This is true even though one or both parties may have expended significant costs in anticipation of the deal. If the deal is not finalized, those sunk costs are simply gone.

As in the agreement to agree situations, however, modern contract law doctrine has recognized certain exceptions to the general rule about precontract liability in circumstances where necessary to prevent injustice. For example, we have already seen, in § D.3.c above, that the *Restatement (Second)* will impose a duty on an offeror to hold open as an option an offer which the offeror should reasonably have expected to induce substantial reliance.

Another area that has generated case significant caselaw in this area involves "letters of intent." This is a device frequently used in more sophisticated transactions—such as the purchase and sale of a business—where the deal involves many discrete points of agreement, all of which must be resolved before the deal is final. Because negotiations to reach complete and final agreement will take a period of time (and often a considerable period of time), at some point during the process, the parties will reduce the points of agreement so far, as well as the items still be negotiated, to writing in order to prevent misunderstanding and, hopefully, pave the way for future agreement.

Usually, these letters of intent will contain a provisions to the effect that, "this letter is not intended to create liability or obligation on the part of either party." While courts will typically respect such a statement of intention not to be legally bound, some cases have found that the letter of intent may give rise to a mutual obligation to continue negotiations in good faith. What this means is that, while the parties are not specifically bound by the terms so far agreed, neither can they simply walk away from further negotiations without making a serious effort to come to agreement as to the remaining terms.

The idea that liability might attach after commencement of negotiations but before the conclusion of a final meeting; i.e., during the precontract formation stage, is at odds with the traditional binary nature of contract liability—either there is a contract or there is not. That traditional model, however, was a product of a simpler time and simpler transactions. Still, in the overwhelming number of cases, liability does not attach until mutual assent has been achieved—either Epstein has agreed to sell Armie, or he hasn't!

Chapter 2

IS THE DEAL ENFORCEABLE? (BASES OF PROMISSORY LIABILITY)

A. CONSIDERATION

1. In General

As noted earlier, no society can afford to or would want to get into the business of enforcing every promise. **The most fundamental limitation on the enforcement of promises under the common law is the requirement of** *consideration.* We were already exposed to the doctrine of consideration in the last chapter and didn't get too sick, so let's take a longer look at this ancient but murky term.

In older cases, you'll notice consideration referred to as consisting of a benefit to the promisor or a detriment to the promise. We never really could make much sense of that formulation, and find the modern definition of consideration to be more penetrable, although not necessarily any clearer in application. **The *Restatement (Second)* defines consideration as something given in *exchange* for the promise that is *bargained-for.*** That "something" could be an act, a promise to do something in the future, or a promise not to do something in the future (i.e., a forbearance). So when Markell promises Ponoroff $20 in return for washing and waxing his car, the promise to pay $20 is the consideration for Ponoroff's services and, in turn, those services are the consideration for Markell's promise to pay $20.

In contrast to the above example, if Markell had promised to give Ponoroff $20 in one week, and Ponoroff accepted, there would be an agreement, but no consideration. Thus, Ponoroff would have to rely on Markell's goodwill and moral conscience for performance. Good luck on that. The point is that nothing was given in exchange for Markell's promise, or, put another way, Markell was not bargaining for anything in exchange for his promise. **The promise was a gift. Generally speaking, gift promises—far less vital to a functioning economy—are not enforceable.**

By the same token, the promise must induce, [i.e., be "bargain for"] the consideration. Thus, if Ponoroff says to Markell, "I'll wash and wax your car for you if you bring it by my house this weekend." Markell's conduct in driving his car to Ponoroff's house is probably not consideration since it is not what induced the promise. Markell's driving was simply something Markell had to do to receive the benefit of a gratuitous promise. We say "probably," because it ultimately comes down to a factual determination in any given case as to whether or not the promise was made in exchange for the detriment incurred by the other party.

Take the famous 1891 case of *Hamer v. Sidway*, which is likely in your casebook. An uncle promises his nephew $5,000 if the nephew will refrain from drinking, swearing, smoking, and gambling until he turns 21. The nephew complied, but the executor for the uncle's estate refused to pay, raising the lack of consideration as a defense. Specifically, the executor claimed the uncle did not benefit from the promise and that nephew did not suffer a detriment because refraining from these activities was actually *good* for him. The New York Court of Appeals disagreed, finding that the detriment necessary to constitute good consideration for a promise is a *legal* not an *actual* detriment. Thus, it was sufficient that that the nephew restricted his lawful freedom of action. Whether the performance of the condition of the promise also constituted a benefit to the uncle was of no moment, since the court found that the benefit/detriment requirements are in the alternative. However, the court hinted that, if necessary, it would have found a benefit in terms of the satisfaction the uncle received from knowing his nephew, who was also his namesake, was leading a virtuous life. In fact, if the promisee incurs a legal detriment, necessarily the promisor has obtained a legal benefit.

In modern terms, it's pretty easy to see that there was a bargain in *Hamer*; i.e., nephew gives up doing things he has a legal right to do (and presumably had done in the past) in exchange for the promise of money. However, short of a situation where the promisee has no legal right to do what he agreed not to do, it's hard to see the doctrine of consideration operating as a very significant limitation on the enforcement of promises, so long as there is some act or return promise given by the promisee. But maybe that's ok, as it is not exactly obvious to us why enforcement of promises should depend on the presence of consideration at all, as opposed to say a written or electronic record, which provides clear evidence of the terms of the promise as well as shows that it was undertaken seriously. Be that as it may, we still have the doctrine and it does emphasize the primacy of *exchange* as a foundational element in the law of contracts.

2. Past Consideration

The term past consideration is a bit of a misnomer. **Past consideration is not consideration**. Something that happened before a promise cannot be consideration for that promise. You cannot bargain for someone to do something she has already done.

Assume that Ponoroff, just because he's a terrific guy, washes and waxes Markell's car. Markell, on seeing what a fine job Ponoroff did, says, "thank you so much; it's a job that's easily worth $50, but since I'm a judge and have no money I can only afford $20, which I'll pay you on Friday when I get my next paycheck."

When Friday arrives, Markell changes his mind and refuses to pay. Will Ponoroff recover if he sues? Under traditional contract theory, the answer is "no," because the promise was essentially a gift. That which might have served as consideration—Ponoroff's services—had already been provided by the time the promise was made. Stated another way, those services did not *induce* the promise; they were not given in exchange for the promise because Ponoroff had finished washing the car before he had any expectation of payment. So, while there might be some divine day of reckoning when Markell will pay for breaking his promise, it's not today. Later, however, in § B, we will discuss some circumstances where past consideration might be regarded as sufficient to support a current promise.

3. Adequacy of Consideration

Courts do not look into the adequacy of consideration, just its existence. Hence the adage that even a mere peppercorn will suffice to satisfy the requirement of consideration. This notion—that relative equivalence of exchange is not a condition to enforcement—is consistent with the principle of freedom of contract and the role of courts as enforcing the private deals struck by the parties; not making or re-making those deals for the parties. In fact, however, courts *do* make adequacy judgments in a variety of ways and for a variety of purposes, including in evaluating several defenses that may be raised, such as unconscionability (as discussed in the next chapter), and for the purpose of making sure that the exchange is not ruse or a sham, as addressed in the next subsection.

4. The Doctrine of Nominal Consideration

Epstein, age 68, has always favored (for reasons no one can understand) his nephew Markell, over his nephew Ponoroff. So, one day, he tells Markell, when I turn 70, I'm going to transfer to you the title to my fully-paid 100 acre estate—known as Epstein Land. Markell is touched, but he's also a calculating little devil who had one year of law school before dropping out to start an internet-based, on-line poker company. So, Markell replies, "Uncle Dave, that's wonderful, I'm so grateful, but would you mind if we arranged this so I paid you $1 in return for Epstein Land." A bit dimwitted, Epstein scratches his head, but decides why not? So that's how the deal is struck. A year later Epstein realizes what a prince Ponoroff is and what a scoundrel Markell is, so he repudiates the earlier promise to sell Epstein Land to Markell for $1. If Markell sues, can Epstein successfully raise the defense of lack of consideration?

The answer, in all likelihood, is "yes." **The *Restatement (Second)*, consistent with the modern formulation of consideration, takes the position that a promise should not be enforced when the purported consideration was not truly bargained-for.**

What about the adage that courts don't inquire into the adequacy of consideration? The reconciliation goes like this. Courts do not require equivalence of exchange, and so if Markell is able through his astute judgment and shrewd bargaining to convince Epstein to part with Epstein Land for a dollar, so be it. However, where the alleged consideration is a sham, and both parties know it—have deliberately disguised what in substance is a gratuitous promise to look like a bargain—enforcement should be denied. In effect, the nominal consideration is significant not because it is inadequate necessarily, but because it serves as a red flag that the true nature of the transaction needs to be scrutinized far more closely.

Sometimes, of course, the promisor may have multiple motives for making the promise, only one of which is to induce the legal detriment to the promise that forms the alleged consideration. Wow, that sentence ought to be shot, huh? Here's what it means. Suppose Epstein, realizing there's not a lot of time left, wants to arrange for the future ownership of Epstein Land. Ideally, he'd like to leave it to his eldest nephew, Markell, so that the property stays in the family. He is also not interested in making money off his nephew, but he'll be damned if he's going to just "give it away." An objective appraiser would probably say Epstein Land is worth $550,000 on the market. So, Epstein offers to sell it to Markell for $300,000. Is the promise to sell supported by consideration? You bet. $300,000 is a real detriment. The fact that the price is very favorable because Epstein has some non-exchange motives in the transaction does not make the promise unenforceable. In cases such as this where the promise is the product of an admixture of motives, only one of which is exchange-based, consideration may be said to exist. It is only when there is no element of exchange—the promise is a gift—that enforcement will fail for lack of consideration.

5. Consideration May Come From or be Received by Third Party

Let us suppose that Markell seeks to borrow money from Ponoroff to buy a new car. After examining Markell's financial situation, Ponoroff refuses to lend on the strength of Markell's credit alone. So Markell approaches Epstein, a foolish but wealthy man, and convinces Epstein to guaranty his debt to Ponoroff, whereupon Ponoroff agrees he will loan the money to Markell. Now ask yourself, what is the consideration for Epstein's promise to stand behind Markell's debt? That's right, it's Ponoroff's agreement to extend credit *to Markell*. And what is the consideration for Ponoroff's promise to lend Markell money? Yup; at least in part, it's *Epstein's* promise to pay the debt if Markell fails to do so. **In terms of the validity of the consideration it does not matter from whom or to whom the benefit and detriment move; what matters is that they are bargained-for and given in exchange for a promise.**

6. Compromise or Surrender of Claims as Consideration

Epstein has sued Markell for $100, claiming that Markell breached his promise to buy Armie, the armadillo. Markell asserts that the promise was contingent on Armie placing at least third in Ponoroff's Armadillo Marathon, where, in fact, Armie finished dead last. Nonetheless, Markell is willing to pay something to avoid the distraction of the lawsuit, so he sends Epstein a letter offering to settle the matter for $20. If Epstein agrees, but Markell later changes his mind and refuses to pay, can Epstein collect the $20? Yes, Markell has promised to pay $20 *in exchange* for Epstein dropping the suit, and the surrender of a *valid* claim constitutes consideration.

Does it matter that Markell did not believe Epstein's claim was valid; or if in fact Epstein's claim was legally invalid? No. **Today, most courts hold that the relinquishment of claim constitutes a detriment, and thus consideration, so long as *either* (i) the claim is objectively well-founded or, (ii) if groundless, the claimant (Epstein, in our example) honestly believes the claim is valid.**

Older common law cases tended to require that the relinquished claim be both reasonable and asserted in good faith. The broad expansion in the enforcement of promises made in return for the release of claims makes sense, and is consistent with the policy favoring the compromise of legitimately disputed claims. It would simply be a disaster if we were to permit the second-guessing of claims surrendered in good faith—private settlements of disputes would never be final.

To illustrate, suppose in a rare moment of generosity, Epstein promises to give Ponoroff a brand new iPad 3. Later, he changes his mind. A disappointed Ponoroff threatens to sue, and just to make him go away, Epstein says, "Ok, I'll pay you $50 to settle this matter." Ponoroff agrees. Does Ponoroff's forbearance from pursuing his claim constitute sufficient consideration to support Epstein's promise. Under the more traditional rule, the answer would likely have been "no," since Ponoroff's claim, based on a pure gift promise, seems untenable on its face. Under the more contemporary view, however, Ponoroff might still prevail if he were able to convince the court that, despite teaching Contracts for 25 years, he had no idea that gift promises were unenforceable and, thus, had a good faith belief in the validity of his claim. Seemingly a tall order, but he could probably get dozens of former students who would testify that he had no idea what he was talking about in class, so who knows?

7. Mutuality of Obligation and Illusory Promises

It's usually pretty easy for students to see how performance operates as consideration. If Ponoroff, induced by Markell's promise of $20, washes and waxes Markell's car (and on a hot and muggy day!) the detriment is clear. Some law students (not ours) have a more difficult time understanding why Ponoroff's mere promise to do the job is consideration, since; after all, Ponoroff has not yet parted with anything of value or provided any service. When you think about it, however, you can quickly see that if executory promises like these, each made in exchange for the other, were not enforceable, our economy would be totally disrupted as no one could depend on the promise of anyone else with respect to future actions and behavior.

It is for this reason that **an exchange of promises typically creates a binding contract, with each party's promise constituting the consideration for the other party's promise.** In other words, if Ponoroff's washing and waxing of Markell's car would constitute good consideration, then so will his promise to perform that same act. In effect, when each party is bound to the other by a promise there is *mutuality of obligation.*

Now, let's adjust our hypothetical just a little and assume that Markell offers Ponoroff $20 to wash and wax Markell's car, and Ponoroff, replies, "Ok, I agree to wash and wax your car if I feel like it." The question then is whether there is consideration for Markell's promise to pay $20. The answer, of course, is "no" because Ponoroff has not committed himself to do anything; there is no mutuality of obligation. Unlike Markell's promise, which is real, Ponoroff's "promise" is said to be *illusory*, because Ponoroff has reserved unbridled discretion over his performance. **When a real promise is exchanged for an illusory promise neither promise is enforceable.** Why not? Think about it before we tell you. That's right, you got it. Markell's real promise is not enforceable because it is not supported by consideration, and Ponoroff's illusory promise is not enforceable because it's not real. How can you be liable for failing to do that which you only agreed to do if the spirit moved you?

Promises based on a condition that cannot occur are also usually deemed illusory for obvious reasons. If it is impossible for the condition to occur, then the promise can and will never be executed. Let's say Ponoroff gives Epstein his favorite Brat Pack box set in exchange for Epstein's promise to pay $300 for it if, by the end of the day, Marilyn Monroe has showed up at Ponoroff's doorstep. Although Ponoroff may not believe this is an impossible condition, it likely is, and it's also likely that a court would find this promise to be illusory, and thus, invalid.

Promises that are on their face illusory because performance appears to be left solely to the option of the promisor might be rendered real, and thus good consideration, by judicial imposition of a limitation on the promisor's unfettered discretion. So, if Ponoroff promises to pay $100 for Epstein's armadillo, Armie, provided he can get a loan to cover the purchase price, courts today will typically imply an obligation on Ponoroff to make a good faith effort to obtain loan approval. This means if Ponoroff never even makes an effort to find and talk to a lender, he cannot use the inability to obtain a loan as grounds to avoid liability for breach of his promise to Epstein.

8. Modification and the Pre–Existing Duty Rule

Let's say Epstein, Markell, and Ponoroff agree to work for Alaska Packers as fishermen during salmon season in remote Alaskan waters for a fixed fee of $5,000. When their ship arrives at its destination in Alaska, they demand that the contract be modified to increase their pay to $10,000 for exactly the same work that they had earlier agreed to do for $5,000. Alaska Packers' representative on board the ship agrees to the contract modification. At the end of the season Alaska Packers refuses to pay more than the $5,000 originally agreed upon. Can Epstein, *et al.* recover for breach of the agreement as *modified*? Under the 1902 decision in *Alaska Packers' Assn v. Domenico*, the answer was "no."

The answer was "no," because the new promise to pay the additional $5,000 was not supported by consideration; Epstein, Markell, and Ponoroff did not agree to do anything beyond what they were already bound to do. **This rule was known as the pre-existing duty rule, which held that a promise to do which a party is already bound to do, or refrain from doing something she has already agreed not to do, could not constitute consideration for a contract modification.** Its application meant that for any contract modification to be enforceable, the modified agreement had to be supported by *new* consideration.

The basis for the rule was a concern that a one-sided modification might be a sign that the modified promise was not truly voluntary, but rather the product of some form of duress; i.e., ordinarily, a person doesn't agree to pay more (or take less) without receiving something in return from the other party, *unless* that person is being pressured improperly. Thus, the requirement of a new consideration helped ensure that the modification had not been coerced.

In *Alaska Packers* the rule seemed to work pretty well. The pre-existing duty rule was, however, much criticized for being over-inclusive. That is to say, it prevented parties to a contractual arrangement from being able to voluntarily modify their performance obligations in light of new circumstances, unanticipated difficulties, etc. Suppose conditions when the ship arrived in Alaskan waters were much harsher than anyone anticipated, and our boys asked for a few extra bucks. Realizing the rate of pay was still well below what it would take for anyone else to do the work in that environment, Alaska Packers says "ok." Under the pre-existing duty rule, that promise was no more enforceable than the one to pay an additional $5,000.

For this reason courts often looked for ways to avoid application of the pre-existing duty rule, such as looking for any new detriment, regardless of how slight, or indulging the fiction that the modification was immediately preceded by the mutual recession of the original deal. If recession occurred, that meant there was a moment in time when neither party was obligated to the other, the consideration for the original deal could serve as the consideration for the modified deal. Eventually, many courts dealt with the problem more directly and simply by holding that if the modification was made in light of unforeseen circumstances and was fair and equitable, it would be enforced despite the absence of consideration. This is the position taken by § 89 of the *Restatement (Second)*.

The UCC goes even further. **In contracts for the sale of goods, Section 2–209 provides simply that an agreement modifying a contract for the sale of goods needs no consideration to be enforceable.** The Official Comment to that section adds, however, that a modification must meet the test of good faith or it is barred.

B. CONSIDERATION SUBSTITUTES (AND MORE)

1. The Material Benefit Rule (Promise + Prior Benefit Conferred)

You will recall that we recently learned that past consideration is not consideration. Like many general rules in contract law, and law generally, however, that's true *except when it's not!* So, let's assume, out of the goodness of his heart, Ponoroff washes and waxes Markell's car. On seeing his gleaming, spiffy car, Markell calls Ponoroff and says, "You did such a great job, it's easily worth $50. I don't have that much, but I am going to give you $20 for your efforts on Friday when I get paid." Ponoroff is thrilled and thanks him, but later Markell, being a little on the cheap side, changes his mind and decides not to pay. As we've seen, because the promise is gratuitous and was not given in exchange for the car wash, it would not be enforceable.

The common law has long-recognized three exceptions to the rule about past consideration. These are a promise to pay:

1. *A debt barred by a statute of limitations:* Epstein lends Ponoroff money that Ponoroff does not repay. Epstein

allows the statute of limitations on this claim to run before bringing suit, but, thereafter, Ponoroff reaffirms his obligation to pay.

2. *A debt discharged in bankruptcy:* Same facts as (1) except Ponoroff receives a discharge in bankruptcy. *Note;* as a matter of federal bankruptcy law, which trumps state law, the reaffirmed debt is *not enforceable.*

3. *A promise to perform a previously voidable obligation*: Ponoroff promises to pay Markell Motors $1,000 for a 1978 VW Rabbit. The promise is induced by fraud: Markell has turned back the odometer and didn't disclose the real mileage. Upon discovering (and in spite of) Markell's fraud, Ponoroff reaffirms the promise to buy the car.

Observe that all three of these situations are different from our example in that there was either previously a legally binding obligation, or a binding obligation subject to a defense. In our case, Markell's promise was made in recognition of a prior event— Ponoroff's car care service. There was never a legal obligation; only a moral obligation and enforcement based purely on moral obligation is inconsistent with the doctrine of consideration.

Of course, there is an exception to this general rule; circumstances where a promise made in recognition of past benefits may be enforceable. This "exception" is known as the "material benefit rule." To understand this rule, we believe it may be helpful first to introduce the concept of a contract "implied in law," and to distinguish that type of "contract" from both an express contract and a contract "implied in fact." The latter two terms refer to true contracts; that is, agreements predicated on the voluntary undertakings of the parties—whether the promises are evidenced by words (express contract) or conduct (implied-in-fact contract). An implied-in-law contract—or quasi-contract—is not really a contract at all. It is an undertaking created under the law of restitution to prevent an unjust enrichment. There is no real promise or voluntary consent; but rather a duty imposed by law to pay for (i.e., make restitution) the value of a benefit conferred on the defendant by the plaintiff so as to avoid an inequity. Being neither promise nor fault-based, a quasi-contract lies somewhere between the law of contracts and torts.

To illustrate, let's assume Ponoroff discovers Epstein's armadillo, Armie, sitting by the back door of Ponoroff's house one morning, injured and in need of immediate medical attention. Ponoroff recognizes Armie, and knows how important he is to Epstein—who is on sabbatical in Timbuktu and cannot easily be reached. So Ponoroff takes Armie and brings him to Markell's Emergency Armadillo Medical Center in Waco. If an appreciative but cheap Epstein refuses to reimburse Ponoroff for the costs he incurred in caring for Armie, Ponoroff has no claim for breach of contract since: (1) there is no promise, and (2) even if there were a promise, it would not supported by good consideration. It is in these circumstances that Ponoroff might be able to maintain a claim in quasi-contract in order to prevent the unjust enrichment of Epstein. Note that if it were Epstein's minor child, Ponoroff would almost surely recover. This is because, even though Epstein might be fonder of the armadillo, he owes the child a support obligation as a matter of law.

Now, if we go back to the car washing example, we see that a claim in restitution for the reasonable value of Ponoroff's services would not be successful. Recovery in restitution is not available for mere "volunteers"; where the benefit is conferred gratuitously without reasonable any reasonable expectation of compensation. Otherwise, Ponoroff would just go around washing and waxing everyone's car and then demanding to be paid. Also, except under emergency circumstances that render it inexpedient to do so (or where the plaintiff performs for the defendant a duty imposed by law on the defendant), a party seeking recovery in quasi-contract must show that the other party was given the opportunity to decline the benefit. On the other hand, our car washing scenario differs from the typical unjust enrichment case in a very important respect; namely, the existence of a *real* promise by Markell to pay for the prior benefit. There is still no consideration to support the promise, but, in these instances, enforcement might obtain under the material benefit rule. It is as if the promise, which does not exist in the quasi-contract situation, cures the impediment (the originally gratuitous nature of the act) to enforcement.

The *Restatement (Second's)* formulation of the material benefit rule in § 86 is a wonderful example of how far contract law has evolved from the cut and dry rules oriented approach of the first *Restatement*. It provides that a promise made in recognition of a prior benefit may be enforced "to the extent necessary to prevent injustice." The promise must also not have been conferred as a gift and must not be disproportionate in value to the benefit conferred. So, can Ponoroff enforce Markell's promise to pay him $20? The answer, of course, is maybe. Is enforcement necessary to prevent injustice? Ponoroff thinks so, do you? Was the benefit conferred as a gift—in honor of Markell's seventh anniversary as a bankruptcy judge—or just gratuitously. Is the value disproportionate to the benefit—probably not—Markell himself said the job was worth $50, but he was too poor (or too cheap) to pay that much, but it's still an issue.

2. Promissory Estoppel (Promise + Unbargained for Reliance)

a. Defined

Sometimes, the bargain-theory of consideration is too narrow and inflexible to achieve equity in all cases. This is true with dealings that fall somewhere between traditional exchange transactions (with clear consideration) and non-exchange donative promises (where consideration is clearly absent). Sometimes these circumstances leave a party who detrimentally changed her position in reliance on a promise in an unduly harsh position, and without a contractual remedy. It is in these circumstances that promissory estoppel may be available as an affirmative basis for enforcement.

Under the doctrine of promissory estoppel, a promise that forseeably induces reliance on the part of the promisee, may be enforced despite the absence of consideration. There are a number of elements to the cause that must be satisfied, including (i) a promise, (ii) justifiable and detrimental reliance on such promise by the promisee that (iii) the promisor should have expected to cause the promisee to change her position by taking some action or forbearing from acting, and (iv) enforcement is necessary to prevent injustice. *Restatement (Second) of Contracts* § 90.

Since all of the above elements must be satisfied to have a promissory estoppel claim, many reliance claims that seem valid actually have no legal basis at all. Let's take a closer look at some of the elements to see what it really takes to establish a valid promissory estoppel claim (it's not as easy as it looks):

The basis of liability under promissory estoppel is more tort-like than contract-like. That is to say, when a promise is enforced because the promisee relied to her detriment, we are, in effect, saying that it would be *wrong* to allow the party that knowingly caused that harm to escape responsibility. In other words, the basis for liability (and recovery) has shifted from promise, which lies at the core of classical contract law, to what is clearly much more of a fault-based rationale.

Example: Epstein promises that he will turn over his share of next year's royalties from *A Short & Happy Guide to Contracts* to Markell. Thrilled, Markell goes out and buys a new Mercedes on credit, assuming he can use Epstein's royalties to pay off the debt.

When Epstein learns what a spendthrift Markell has been, he refuses to turn over his share of the royalties when the big, fat checks from West Academic Publishing arrive. Clearly, the promise is donative and cannot be enforced under traditional contract theory. Might Markell recover, however, under promissory estoppel? Maybe—not all gift promises on which there has been reliance are enforceable. It will require a factual determination of whether Epstein should have foreseen reliance on his promise and whether non-enforcement would work an injustice.

b. Distinguished From Equitable Estoppel

Students frequently get equitable and promissory estoppel mixed up (Epstein does, too, but in his case it's probably due to old age and creeping senility). This is understandable, as promissory estoppel evolved from the older concept of equitable estoppel, and both involve an "estoppel," which means to bar or prohibit one from doing something. However, promissory estoppel and equitable estoppel are quite different. **Equitable estoppel is a defense that exists throughout the fabric of the law; it is not related just to contract cases. It is invoked to bar a person, who misstates certain facts, from later asserting the truth of the matter earlier misrepresented against a party that relied to her detriment on the first statement.**

Assume Epstein owes Ponoroff $1,000, which is to be paid in twenty equal monthly installments of $50 each payable on or before the first day of each month. For the first sixth months, Epstein's payments always arrive by the first of the month. Before the beginning of the seventh month, Epstein calls Ponoroff and asks him if it would be alright if the next payment was a few days late. Ponoroff replies, "Sure, as long as the monthly payment comes in before the 10th of the month, that would be fine." Relieved, Epstein, who is bit stretched financially, but could have made the payment on the first day of the seventh month, waits to pay until he receives his paycheck on the fifth of the month. Thereupon, Ponoroff declares the obligation to be in default due to the failure to make timely payment of all installments, and brings suit to collect the full amount of the debt still outstanding.

On these facts, Epstein might well be successful in estopping Ponoroff from using the original due date of the first of the month as a basis to prove a default. Because Epstein was reasonable in believing that Ponoroff was allowing him a 10–day grace period, and altered his position in a significant way based on Epstein's statement, it would now be inequitable to allow Ponoroff to claim a default based on the late payment. *Note:* Epstein might also argue a valid modification of the original promise, despite the absence of consideration.

By contrast to equitable estoppel, promissory estoppel is based not on a false statement of past or present fact, but a promise relating to future behavior. It is also not raised as a defense to a claim by another, but rather as an affirmative basis for imposing liability on the promisor. As discussed in the next two subsections, promissory estoppel originally developed as a substitute for consideration in situations involving gift promises, but it has gradually been expanded to represent a separate basis of promissory liability in cases that do not involve an enforceable deal for reasons *other than* the absence of a bargain transaction.

c. As a Substitute for Consideration

Early on in the development of the doctrine of promissory estoppel, and even still in the view of a few courts, the doctrine was reserved for cases that did not involve run-of-the-mill commercial transactions in which an exchange would be expected. Rather, it was limited to those cases that, by their nature, did not involve bargain transactions. This might involve promises made in the course of familial or social relationships, and, more famously, promises made to charitable organizations (so-called "charitable subscriptions"). Courts were reluctant to allow people who made big pledges to charities to walk away from those promises without legal consequence, but these promises were by definition gratuitous. Rather than stretch the doctrine of consideration beyond all recognizable bounds (which sometimes happened), courts began to employ promissory estoppel as a basis for enforcement in these cases.

The difficulty in many cases, however, was in finding reliance on the promise. Section 90(2) of the *Restatement (Second)*, therefore, takes the position that charitable subscriptions should be enforced without regard to reliance, but based simply on the existence of the promise.

Today, a few courts still take the view that promissory estoppel is limited to cases where all other elements of a contract exist save for consideration. These courts maintain that where consideration exists, but some other impediment to enforcement is present, there is no gap for promissory estoppel to fill, even though the plaintiff may have relied on the defendant's promise in a manner that now renders enforcement the only way to prevent injustice. The majority of courts, however, follow the view that promissory estoppel is more than just a proxy for consideration and, in fact, represents an alternative theory on which liability for non-performance of promises may be based. This expansion of the doctrine has brought promissory estoppel into mainstream business and commercial transactions, as we turn to next.

d. As an Independent Basis of Liability

Let's suppose that Epstein, the managing partner in Epstein, Lawless, & Faultless Firm ("ELF") located in Richmond, offers Markell a highly paid position in the firm. Excited by the prospect of finally making some "real money," Markell resigns from the bench, sells his house, buys a house in Richmond, packs up, and moves. Upon arriving in Richmond, Epstein advises Markell that his services are no longer required since ELF has just successfully recruited Ponoroff to occupy the position that Markell would have held. Now, there is a contract here that is supported by consideration, but Markell doesn't have much of a case against ELF, since this was an employment "at will," meaning it was terminable at the pleasure of the employer. Markell relied upon Epstein's promise by quitting his existing job, selling his house, etc., and it seems unjust to leave him without a remedy. It is in this type of circumstance that Markell might sustain a claim based on promissory estoppel to at least recover some of the losses and expenses incurred as a result of relying on Epstein's offer of employment.

In the last chapter, you may recall that we saw that foreseeable reliance on a promise can be a basis to hold an offer open as an option contract for a reasonable time. That rule is another extension of the doctrine of promissory estoppel. In addition, on occasion promissory estoppel has been employed to permit recovery based on promises or assurances made during the course of pre-contract negotiations. The most famous of these cases, which may even be in your casebook, is the 1965 Wisconsin Supreme Court decision in *Hoffman v. Red Owl Stores, Inc.* In that case, the Court awarded out-of-pocket expense damages against a grocery store franchisor that had made certain assurances to a prospective franchisee during the course of their negotiations. Those negotiations never ripened into a binding contract, but the plaintiff incurred expenses in reasonable reliance on the defendant's assurances of a new franchise, and the Court felt it would be unjust not to hold the franchisor responsible for those costs.

e. Remedies in Promissory Estoppel Cases

An interesting question is whether the damages in a promissory estoppel case should be calculated in the same fashion as damages in a traditional breach of contract case. The *Restatement (Second)* simply says that "damages may be limited as justice requires." But how helpful is that? The question arises because in the typical breach of contract scenario we are saying to the breacher, "you broke your promise, so you have to make good on it by giving the other party the benefit of its bargain." This requires, as we will discuss in Chapter 6, *expectation* damages. In the promissory estoppel situation, we are saying, "the plaintiff has been harmed and it's your fault." This suggests the remedy should be, as in tort law, to compensate the plaintiff for the loss caused by the detrimental change in position occasioned by reliance on the promise. These would be *reliance* damages.

It may be easier to understand this distinction with a simple example. Let's go back to the example where Epstein promises to convey title to his estate—Epstein Land—to his nephew, Markell, in five years. Now let's assume that, in anticipation of becoming the owner of Epstein Land, Markell builds a fine new house on the back forty acres. If Epstein fails to perform as promised, he clearly has a defense of failure of consideration should Markell sue. Markell might, however, very well prevail on a promissory estoppel claim since, arguably, we have reasonable and foreseeable detrimental reliance on Epstein's promise. The question then becomes, what remedy should the court grant Markell if his promissory estoppel action is successful. Should it make Epstein transfer title to the property (expectation) or reimburse Markell for the costs he incurred in building the new house on Epstein Land (reliance)? The answer is that there is really no definitive answer (by now, this shouldn't surprise you).

One point that does seem fairly clear is that when promissory estoppel is being asserted to enforce a promise made either during the course of preliminary negotiations or as part of an agreement that is not enforceable other than because of an absence of consideration, it is usually appropriate to restrict damages to losses resulting from, or expenses incurred by the plaintiff in, reliance on the promise. This is essentially the result in the example above where Epstein breached his promise of a position for Markell in Epstein, Lawless, & Faultless. When promissory estoppel is invoked as a substitute for consideration, there is perhaps a stronger case for an expectation remedy (full scale enforcement of the promise), but, once more, the matter is still the subject of some debate and disagreement.

f. A Caution (or Two)

We have all been teaching Contracts a long time, although, because of his age, Epstein longest of all. Over that time, we have seen students become quite smitten with promissory estoppel—to the point that when the time comes for the exam they see it everywhere! So we caution you that before jumping to promissory estoppel as a solution to a problem (or an exam question), you should see if a typical contract—one supported by consideration—exists. If so, it is almost invariably unnecessary to reach for promissory estoppel. Similarly, even in jurisdictions that recognize promissory estoppel as an independent, almost tort-like theory of liability, recognize that there are several elements to a successful claim under the theory and that, more often than not in the "real world," promissory estoppel claims fail because not every element can be satisfied. So, particularly in a Contracts course, when you have enforcement of a contract being challenged for whatever reason, such as lack of mutual assent, indefiniteness, absence of a writing, etc., first examine the traditional rules of contract law to sustain enforcement of the promise before running headlong into the argument that it doesn't matter because of promissory estoppel. In short, think of promissory estoppel as the exception, not the rule.

———

Just because you have an enforceable deal does not mean you automatically win. It just means you'll get your day in court. The next issue to consider is whether the defendant has a good *defense* to enforcement. That's where we turn next.

Chapter 3

ARE THERE DEFENSES
TO ENFORCEMENT
OF THE DEAL?

You now know that a contract is an agreement that is legally enforceable and that lack of consideration or a consideration substitute is one of the reasons that an agreement is not legally enforceable. Next, we need to learn about other reasons that an agreement is not legally enforceable.

Some of these reasons—commonly referred to as "defenses"—are based on (i) the form of the agreement (i.e., whether there is a signed writing), or (ii) flaws in the agreement process (i.e., what happened before the agreement), or (iii) the content of the agreement. (i.e., what the agreement says). Still other reasons for not enforcing the agreement—commonly referred to as "excuses"—are based on what happens after the contract. We will cover excuses later, in Chapter 6.

A. DEFENSE BASED ON THE FORM OF THE AGREEMENT (STATUTE OF FRAUDS)

The defense that appears most often in first-year contracts exam questions is the statute of frauds defense.[1] **Under the statute of frauds, certain agreements must be, if not actually in writing, then at least evidenced by writing, in order to be enforceable.** This brings to mind the wisecrack by former

---

1. Some people capitalize the "Statute of Frauds." Do what your professor does.

Hollywood mogul Louie B. Mayer, who reportedly once quipped that "an oral agreement isn't worth the paper it's written on."

In the "real world", virtually any agreement of sufficient substance to warrant lawyer involvement will be in writing. Nonetheless, because it is so easy for your professor to write a statute of frauds issue into her exam questions, you need to be able to answer four questions about the statute of frauds: (1) what is the purpose of the statute of frauds, (2) which agreements are covered by (i.e., "within") the statute of frauds (3) does the writing meet the requirements ("satisfy") the statute of frauds and (4) when is an agreement within the statute of frauds enforceable without a writing?

1. What Is the Purpose of the Statute of Frauds?

England adopted a statute of frauds in the 17th century to prevent false claims by an unethical plaintiff that there was an oral agreement when, in reality, there was no such agreement. Legislatures in all states have enacted similar statutes. England abolished the statute of frauds more than 50 years ago to prevent false claims by an unethical defendant that there was no oral agreement when, in reality, there was such an agreement. Our legislatures have not abolished their statutes of frauds. Courts, however, consistently interpret statutes of frauds in ways that limit the statutes' scope and impact.

2. Which Agreements are Covered by (i.e. "Within") the Statute of Frauds?

With the exception of § 2–201 of the UCC, statutes of frauds vary from state to state in terms of what types of agreements are covered. **Most states' statutes of fraud, and, more important, most contracts casebooks' coverage of the statute of frauds include: (i) transfers of interests in real estate, (ii) services contracts not capable of being performed within a year of the date of the contract, and (iii) sales of goods for $500 or more.**

With respect to real estate transfers, notice that the purchase price is irrelevant to the question of whether the statute of frauds applies to the deal. Thus, an agreement to transfer an easement for $1 has to be in writing. By contrast, with respect to sales of goods, the purchase price is determinative. *All* that is relevant to the question of whether the statute of frauds applies is the purchase price (and the relevant number is $500 because Article 2 is a product of the 1950's).

Most of the law school questions about whether the agreement is covered by the statute of frauds involve services contracts. And, here are the kinds of questions to watch for:

    a.   *Fixed time period:* Is a contract to provide landscaping services for two years "within" the statute of frauds even though the contract provides that either party can terminate the agreement on five days notice? Generally "yes." Most statutes of frauds focus only on whether the agreement can be "performed" within a year and treat termination as different from performance. A two-year agreement, by definition, cannot be performed in the space of one year. No way, no how.

    b.   *Fixed time:* Is a January 2, 2012, contract by Kinky Friedman to perform at Madonna's son Rocco's bar mitzvah on August 13, 2013 "within the statute of frauds" even though the Kinkster's performance will only last an hour? "Yes." The focus is not on how long a person actually performs but whether her performance can be completed within a year of the date of the contract. Watch for the exam question that gives you both the date of the contract and the date that the contract specifies performance must occur.

    c.   *Task:* Is a contract by Markell to move the Statute of Liberty to Las Vegas within the statute of frauds? No. Contracts for the performance of a specific task, as contrasted with contracts for a specific time period or a specific time are never within the statute of frauds. The amount of time that it will take Markell to perform is irrelevant. Most statute of frauds regarding service contracts use language similar to "capable of being performed within a year of the date of the contract." And most courts interpret the word "capable" in this context as meaning "theoretically possible with unlimited resources." With unlimited resources, any task, including moving the Statute of Liberty to Las Vegas is "capable" of being performed within a year of the date of the contract.

    d.   *Lifetime:* Ponoroff offers Epstein a contract for lifetime employment, is it within the statute of frauds. No. The agreement is capable of being fully performed without breach within the space of one year because Epstein may die after six months. Note: this would be true even if Epstein weren't really old.

3. If There Is a Writing, Does the Writing Satisfy the Statute of Frauds?

To determine whether a writing meets the requirements of (i.e., satisfies) a statute of frauds, look to the contents of the writing and also to who signed the writing.

a. Contents

Statutes of fraud vary greatly in terms of what terms must be in the writing. An exam question that questions whether the contents of the writing meet the requirements of the statute of frauds will either (i) quote the language of the statute or (ii) involve a sale of goods. In the former case, just compare the language of the statute with the facts of the question. **Under § 2–201, the only term which must appear in the writing is the quantity term, e.g., 17 widgets. Section 2–201 does not require that the price be set out in writing.**

b. Who Signed the Writing

Generally, a writing that satisfies the statute of frauds must be signed by the defendant—in the language of the UCC statute of frauds, § 2–201, "the party against whom enforcement is sought." That makes sense. How would a writing signed only by the plaintiff address the statute of frauds' concern that the plaintiff was falsely claiming an agreement when in reality there was no agreement?

Section 2–201(2) creates a very limited exception—describes a very specific fact situation in which a writing signed by the *plaintiff* satisfies the statute of frauds. Section 2–201(2) is limited to (i) sale of goods in which (ii) both the buyer and seller are "merchants" (as that term is defined in § 2–104), and (iii) the recipient of a signed writing "in confirmation of the contract" fails to object in writing within 10 days.

For example, Ponoroff send Markell a letter signed by Ponoroff stating, "This is to confirm that we have agreed that you are selling me Armie the armadillo with payment to be made on delivery." Markell does not object to the letter; Markell does not send the armadillo. If Ponoroff sues Markell for breach of contract, Markell will not have a statute of frauds defense. Under § 2–201(2), even though the only writing was signed by Ponoroff the plaintiff, the statute of frauds was satisfied by Markell's failure to object to the writing.

More important than understanding the particulars of § 2–201(2) is understanding the limited importance of § 2–201(2). Saying that under § 2–201(2) Markell loses the statute of frauds defense is *very different* from saying that Markell loses the lawsuit. Ponoroff still has the burden of proof on all of the elements of his breach of contract claim—including the burden of proving that there was indeed a contract.

4. When Is an Agreement Within the Statute of Frauds Enforceable Without a Writing?

a. Part Performance

Some statutes of frauds expressly provide for a part performance exception to the statute of frauds. Section 2–201(3) (a) and 2–201(3) (c) are examples of such a statute.

In some other instances, courts have recognized part performance exceptions to the statute of frauds. For example, in many states, an oral agreement to transfer an interest in land is enforceable if the buyer/plaintiff can prove any two of the following three facts: (1) payment of all or part of the purchase price, (2) possession of the land, and/or (3) improvements to the land. Such judicially created exceptions to a statute raise (hopefully) obvious questions about the relative roles of legislatures and courts insofar as the making and interpreting of law is concerned.

b. Reliance

Restatement (Second) § 139 provides that an oral promise can be enforceable because of reliance, notwithstanding the statute of frauds. For example, on April 15, D, a company in Hawaii, orally agrees to employ P, a California resident, for one year, starting July 13. P moves to Hawaii and starts work on July 13. D terminates P, without cause, on December 3. P sues for breach of contact, and D assets a statute of frauds defense. Under *Restatement (Second)* § 139, D's oral promise would enforceable because of reliance, notwithstanding the statute of frauds.

In a sense § 139 is an adaption of promissory estoppel in relation to statutes of frauds. Unlike § 90 of the *Restatement (Second),* § 139 has not yet been widely adopted or applied.

Review: **The three most important things for you to remember about the statute of frauds are: (i) not all agreements** must be in writing: some agreements are not within the statute of frauds; in some situations, an agreement within the statute of frauds is enforceable without a writing; (ii) not all writing satisfy the statute of frauds; and (iii) the defendant's losing on its statute of frauds defense does *not* mean that the defendant has lost the case, because the plaintiff still has the burden of proving that there was a contract, and the defendant may still have other defenses such as duress, misrepresentation, concealment, mistake, or unconscionability. . . .

B. DEFENSES BASED ON FLAWS IN THE AGREEMENT PROCESS

1. Duress

"Gun to the head" duress—e.g., Epstein's contracting to sell his 1973 Cadillac to Ponoroff because Ponoroff was threatening to shoot Epstein's dog—is a defense to enforcement based on the agreement process. But it is unlikely that you will see questions concerning physical duress on your contracts final because they are too easy.

A more likely exam question is an economic duress fact pattern similar to *Alaska Packers Ass'n v. Domenico*, discussed in Chapter 2 in connection with enforcement of contract modifications: Epstein, Markell and Ponoroff agree to work for Alaska Packers as fishermen during salmon season in Alaska for fixed fee of $5,000.each. When they arrive in Alaska, they refuse to work unless their pay is increased to $10,000 for exactly the same work that they had earlier agreed to do for $5,000. Alaska Packers agrees to the contract modification because Epstein, Markell and Ponoroff were irreplaceable. At the end of the season, Alaska Packers refuses to pay more than the $5,000 originally agreed upon. Epstein, *et al,* sue for breach of contract. Under similar facts, the Ninth Circuit ruled for Alaska Packers because there was no consideration for Alaska Packers' to increase the payment from $5,000 to $10,000. Some professors (yours?) believe that the Ninth Circuit should have ruled for Alaska Packers not because of lack of consideration for the modified promise, but because of economic duress based on (1) an improper threat by Epstein, Markell, and Ponoroff to breach unless their pay was increased, and (2) Alaska Packers had no reasonable alternative but to accede to the demand.

There are not many reported cases holding that contract performance is excused by economic duress. This is because in most situations, it's perfectly ok to capitalize on one's economic advantage. [Two of your co-authors claim that Tea Party members say that is what America is all about!] **Thus, the few cases that do recognize a defense based on economic duress emphasize the need for finding _both_ that (1) the person trying to enforce the contract applied wrongful pressure, and (2) the person trying to avoid enforcement of the contract had no reasonable alternative.**

2. Misrepresentation of Existing Facts

Ponoroff is interested in buying a wooden building from Markell but is concerned about possible termite damage. Markell assures Ponoroff that the building has no termites. Ponoroff enters into a contract to buy the building. Subsequent to contracting with Markell but before the contract is performed; Ponoroff learns that the building has been infested with termites for years. The agreement will not be enforceable against Ponoroff if he can establish that Markell's false statement as to existing facts (the non-existence of termites) induced him to enter into the contract.

If, as here, the misrepresentation is also material, then Ponoroff will not have to prove that Markell's misrepresentation was fraudulent or even negligent. **Even innocent misrepresentations _as to existing facts_ can make a contract _voidable._**

Be careful to distinguish between contract actions to void an agreement because of false statement of existing facts and tort actions to collect money damages from loss resulting from misrepresentation. In the tort action, the plaintiff must prove that the person making the misrepresentation knew it was false or, at least, was reckless in ascertaining the truth or falsity of the statement.

Be careful as well to distinguish between misrepresentations of existing facts—e.g., a statement that building has no termites when in fact it does—from broken promises as to what will happen in the future—e.g., a statement that a building will have no termites for the three-year period following the contract and termites infest the building months later. Broken promises are: (a) a basis for recovering damages for breach of contract, and (b) if material, a basis for excuse of future performance, as discussed in Chapter 5.

3. Non-disclosure/Concealment

Non-disclosure without concealment is generally irrelevant. A person making a contract is not required by contract law to tell the other person all that he knows, even if he knows that the other person lacks knowledge of certain facts. And, so, Epstein has no contract law obligation to tell Markell that there is a hole in the floor his 1973 Cadillac when he sells the Cadillac to Markell. If, on the other hand, however, Epstein goes further and conceals the hole by placing a floor mat over it, his nondisclosure coupled with concealment is treated the same as a misrepresentation; that is to say, it is a defense to the enforcement of the agreement available to Markell.

4. Mistake of Existing Facts

In learning about duress, misrepresentation, and concealment, we have seen how "tacky" conduct by one person during the agreement process can make the agreement unenforceable by that person. Mistake is factually distinguishable from duress, misrepresentation, and concealment because mistake cases do not involve tacky behavior.

So, if Markell is arguing that his agreement with Ponoroff is not enforceable because of mistake, Markell is not arguing that he should be able to get out of the deal because Ponoroff did something tacky. Rather, Markell is in essence arguing that he (Markell) should be able to get out of the deal because he (Markell) somehow on his own got a wrong-headed idea about then-existing facts. Understandably, it is and should be harder to get out of an agreement because of your own mistake than it is to get out of an agreement because of the other party's tacky behavior.

a. Mutual mistake

There is a body of case law, and a *Restatement (Second)* provision (§ 152), that support the proposition that if there is a mutual mistake of material fact, then the agreement is voidable by the adversely affected party. So if Markell and Ponoroff contract for the sale of the Markell's cow, Rose, for the low price of $80 because "both parties supposed that the cow was barren" when, at worst, Rose was simply somewhat shy, then Markell can rescind the agreement if the mistake was material. At least, that is what the court said in the famous mutual mistake case of *Sherwood v. Walker*.

And, here is some of what other professors have said about Sherwood v. Walker:

— The majority opinion got the facts wrong: The parties were simply unsure as to whether Rose was barren—not mistaken in the legal sense. Conscious ignorance, not legal mistake.

— The majority opinion got the law wrong: Whether a mistake is material should depend simply on the impact of the mistake on the parties, not on whether the mistake "went to the whole substance of the agreement ... not the mere quality of the animal."

— It is reasonable that Markell should bear the risk of his mistake.

In sum, even if both contracting parties have the same misunderstanding of the facts, courts will deny relief if, (i) the court concludes that there was simply a bad judgment or ignorance instead of "legal mistake," or (ii) there is a mutual mistake but it is not "material," or (iii) there is a material mutual mistake but "under the circumstances," the person seeking relief because of the mistake should bear the risk of his or her mistake.

b. Unilateral mistake

It is even more difficult to obtain rescission in situations in which only the person trying to get out the deal was mistaken— e.g., Markell is mistaken about whether Rose is barren but Ponoroff knows better. *Restatement (Second)* § 53 adds the requirement "enforcement of the contract would be unconscionable." This is because the whole point of contract law is that, to a point, each party is supposed to try to maximize his advantage in the deal at the expense of the other.

The strongest case for relief for unilateral mistake is when there is a clerical or mathematical error, particularly when the error is fairly obvious. For example, suppose that Markell submits the winning bid on building a new bathroom for Ponoroff's office, but mistakenly omits a major cost item from the total. Ponoroff likes the price and promptly accepts. If Markell discovers his unilateral mistake before Ponoroff relies on the contract in some substantial way, Markell can reform or rescind his bid.

C. DEFENSES BASED ON WHAT THE AGREEMENT SAYS

1. Illegality

It is easy to think about agreements that are illegal and understand why the agreement is unenforceable. For example, Markell contracts with Ponoroff to kill Epstein for $1.98. The agreement would be unenforceable by either Markell or Ponoroff. It is against the law to kill someone—even Epstein. This means not only that Markell cannot get specific performance or damages; it also means that, if he paid in advance, he cannot get his $1.98 back from Ponoroff. This is because in a case of illegality where both parties are culpable, the rule is that the court will "leave them where it finds them."

The law in question does not have to be a criminal law. You know and understand that a court will not enforce an agreement to pay 12% interest if the usury statute in the state where the contract was made provides that contracts to pay greater than 10% interest are void.

A harder problem is presented by a statute such as a licensing act that does not expressly provide that contracts in violation of the statute are void. To illustrate: a state statute requires that a person have a plumbing license before installing a plumbing fixture. Ponoroff enters into a contract with Markell, who is not a licensed plumber to install a urinal in his office. Markell does the work. Ponoroff, of course, refuses to pay, asserting that the agreement is unenforceable on the grounds of illegality,

The fact that Markell acted illegally does not necessarily mean that the agreement is unenforceable. Courts look to the policy served by the licensing law. If, for example, a license could be obtained by anyone who paid the licensing fee so that the purpose of licensing was to raise revenue, rather than to protect the public by regulating conduct, the contract might be enforced, notwithstanding Markell's illegal actions.

2. Public Policy

Some courts and commentators, and *Restatement (Second)* § 178, consider illegality as a part of the defense of public policy. More important, courts, commentators, and the *Restatement* recognize that the defense of public policy is not limited to agreements that directly or even indirectly violate a legislative enactment. Public policy can be determined by case law. So if Markell pays Ponoroff $10 to vote in a certain fashion, and Ponoroff fails to do so, a court will refuse to enforce the agreement because purchasing votes for money violates public policy. There is considerable case law on whether a covenant not to compete is unenforceable because of the public policy defense. Covenants not to compete are fairly common in contracts for the sale of business and also employment contracts.

For example, Markell buys a tavern from Epstein and wants assurances that Epstein is not opening a competing tavern in the same neighborhood. Or, restaurant owner Epstein might want assurances that his featured chef, Ponoroff, will not go to work for a competitor should he (Ponoroff) terminate his employment relationship with Epstein.

Lawsuits challenging the enforceability of a covenant not to compete are fairly common. The holding of a particular case depends in the main on facts relating to the reasonableness of the business need for the protective agreement and the reasonableness of the duration and geographic scope of the protective agreement. More generally, the covenant not to compete decisions typically discuss and balance the public policies of (1) freedom of contract, (2) restraint of trade, (3) freedom to compete, and (4) the right of an employee to earn a livelihood.

D. UNCONSCIONABILITY

Both common law and the UCC recognize unconscionability as a defense to the enforcement of an agreement. While both *Restatement (Second)* § 208 and UCC § 2–302 use the word "unconscionable," neither define it.

Here are the four most important points for you to remember about unconscionability:

1. Courts can use the unconscionability doctrine to find that the entire agreement is unenforceable or courts can use the unconscionability doctrine to find that a specific term in the agreement is unenforceable but the remainder of the agreement is enforceable. For example, Markell agrees to paint Ponoroff's Tucson house, Ponoroff agrees to pay $5,000. Markell's standard form agreement provides that all disputes will be resolved by an international arbitration forum in Kazakhstan. A court could find that the arbitration class was unconscionable but that the remainder of the agreement was enforceable.

2. Most courts use the term "procedural unconscionability" in referring to problems with the agreement process and the term "substantive unconscionability" in referring to problems with the terms of the contract. Neither *Restatement (Second)* § 208 nor UCC § 2–302 uses these terms. The Official Comment to § 2–302 does use (i) the phrase "prevention of oppression," which courts have come to equate with oppressive terms and substantive unconscionability, and (ii) the phrase "unfair surprise," which courts have come to equate with procedural unconscionability. You should use the terms "procedural unconscionability" and "substantive unconscionability" in any exam answer that you write about unconscionability.

3. In writing an exam answer about substantive unconscionability, you need to remember that both the Restatement

and the UCC expressly provide that unconscionability is to be tested as of the time of the agreement. Whether terms are oppressive thus turns on whether the terms were fair at the time of the agreement, not months or years later.

4. While the determination of whether a contract or a contract term is unconscionable depends on the relevant facts, the determination is made as a matter of law. The UCC expressly so provides, and cases applying the common law of unconscionability generally so hold.

In summary, when addressing a question about the enforceability of an agreement, look for information about the agreement process. Compare these facts with the facts of the duress, misrepresentation, nondisclosure and procedural unconscionability cases you have studied. Look also for information about the terms of the agreement. Compare these facts with the facts of the illegality, public policy and substantive unconscionability cases that you have studied.

Chapter 4

WHAT ARE THE TERMS OF THE DEAL (PAROL EVIDENCE; INTERPRETATION)?

A. THE IMPORTANCE OF DETERMINING THE "TERMS" OR "PROVISIONS" OF A CONTRACT

Once you know that you have a binding contract, it should be easy to figure if someone's breached it, right? You just look at the terms agreed upon and compare them to what the parties actually did. But while initially alluring, that view is far too simplistic. Contract law has evolved beyond simply looking at only the words the parties actually used. Not surprisingly, it has also developed rules for figuring out what a contract says when the parties use ambiguous words, or when they incompletely express their deal.

Outline the basic strategy. Before determining whether there has been a breach, a court has to figure out what the terms of the deal are. For some terms, or provisions, this is simple. When Ponoroff writes "I agree to sell Armie the Armadillo to Epstein for $25," and Epstein writes "Agreed" on the paper, we know what is being sold—Armie—and the price—$25. That might seem enough.

But when is the deal to be done? And where? And what if Epstein refuses to pay because *everybody* knows that armadillos are only sold if the seller can produce a recent veterinarian certification, and Ponoroff has none? And, finally, what if Epstein refuses to cough up the $25 because he claims that Ponoroff also agreed to throw in the diamond-studded collar Armie was wearing last time Epstein saw him?

Let's take the last problem first. What's wrong with Epstein claiming that the deal was more than just an armadillo for money? That is, what's wrong with claiming the deal is more than just what the paper says? That's where the parol evidence rule comes in.

1.   The Parol Evidence Rule

The parol evidence rule can be tough, starting with its name. First, it is not a rule of evidence. It is a rule of substantive law about what terms and obligations survive the formation of a contract. What does this mean? It means that if the parol evidence rule applies, all prior obligations and terms that related to the contract are *discharged*; that is, satisfied and deemed paid. Over and done with. No longer binding.

You can see this through a simple example. Ponoroff agrees with Epstein to pay $50 for Armie. Later, before performance is due, Ponoroff and Epstein agree that Epstein will buy Ponoroff's Yugo for $2,000, and Ponoroff will throw in (literally) Armie in the deal. The paper they sign says this is the complete deal between them on all points. All shake hands and seal the deal. When the time comes to deliver the car and Armie, Ponoroff demands $2,050—the $2,000 for the car and the $50 for Armie. He thinks there are two contracts; one for Armie, one for the Yugo.

But he will lose. When the second deal was struck for the Yugo, and that deal included Armie, the parol evidence rule *discharged* the first contract. Ponoroff is now stuck with the payment agreed under the second contract only. Let's see how the rule is stated to get to this result.

2.   The Basic Rule

Section 213 of the *Restatement (Second) of Contracts*, which restates the parol evidence rule, says two things. First, it says that a "binding integrated agreement discharges prior agreements to the extent that it is consistent with them." Second, it says that a "binding completely integrated agreement discharges prior agreements to the extent that they are within its scope." As both of these rules use the term "integrated agreement," we need to understand what "integrated agreement" means.

An integrated agreement is one that is complete and final. Duh. But "agreement" here is slippery. It can mean an agreement on just one term in the contract—the subject of the sale contract or the price being paid, for example—or it can refer to the entire set of promises that comprise the contract by which Armie is to be sold. So the first contract above—Armie the Armadillo for $25—is integrated as to its subject—Armie—and its price—$25. If written (and by the way, the parol evidence rule applies *only* to agreements in writing), then this agreement is *partially integrated*.

What does that mean? It means that the formation of that contract did not discharge prior agreements as to matters *other than* price and subject. Say for example that Ponoroff, before signing, said "Let's make the exchange next Tuesday over breakfast," and that Epstein agreed. They then signed the paper without including this term. But its omission does not mean it is not a term of the contract, and when Ponoroff sleeps through the breakfast after going on a bender, Epstein can introduce evidence of the conversation in his breach of contract action without violating the parol evidence rule. To use legalese, the contract was partially integrated as to price and subject, but not completely integrated.

The result would be different, however, if instead of mentioning delivery time, Epstein had said, just before Ponoroff inked the deal, "How about $20, instead of $25?" and Ponoroff replied "Yeah, whatever." Assume that neither bothered to note this change in the final written contract; it still unambiguously states that the price is $25. Here, the price term is integrated because it is an express term of the written contract. So when Epstein tries to weasel out of the $25 and pay only $20, Ponoroff can invoke the parol evidence rule to bar Epstein from introducing any evidence of the pre-formation price discussion. Why? Because even if there was a deal on price different than the written terms, when Ponoroff and Epstein signed the contract, the parol evidence rule discharged all prior deals on price, including the revised deal at $20. The written contract is the beginning and the end of the discussion as to its integrated terms (such as, in this case, price).

So much for the first part of the *Restatement (Second)* and partially integrated terms. What about the second part involving completely integrated agreements? Section 213 purports to discharge all prior agreements within the scope of the written agreement so long as it is "completely integrated." Appreciate what this means. If applicable, then the breakfast exchange over price would *not* be a term of the agreement, as it was with the *scope* of the agreement; and, roughly speaking, something is within the scope of an agreement if it would naturally have been included in the final expression of that deal if it had been part of the deal. (Price is almost always within the scope of the agreement under this test).

This is a big deal. Although a party can introduce evidence of consistent additional or supplementary terms in a *partially* integrated agreement, he or she *cannot* do that with a *completely* integrated one. The completely integrated agreement is what it is, and no more.

So what is "completely integrated"? The *Restatement (Second)* says that a completely integrated agreement is one that reasonably appears to be, in view of its completeness and specificity, a complete statement of the terms related to the deal. The UCC takes a slightly different tack and asks if the term being offered, if agreed upon, would certainly have been included in the parties' final agreement. *See* Comment 3 to UCC § 2–202.

Regardless of what law applies, courts look for "integration" or "merger" clauses in this quest, such as "This agreement is a complete expression of the parties' understanding of the terms of this deal" or "This writing contains all of the terms related to the subject matter of this deal." If such a statement is present, it is a good bet that a court will usually find that the writing is completely integrated—although not always. The test, as stated above, is a functional one: would the deal have been signed without the term being offered?

Take the following example. Epstein agrees with Ponoroff to sell Armie the Armadillo for $50. They both sign a paper that says "Ponoroff agrees to sell, and Epstein agrees to buy, Armie the Armadillo for $50. Payment and Armie to be exchanged next Saturday at 5:00 p.m. at Ponoroff's house. This writing contains all of the terms of this agreement." Epstein shows up at Ponoroff's house at the appointed time, and is outraged that Ponoroff isn't including Armie's diamond-studded collar. "You said you'd include it when we first started talking about the deal!" moans Epstein. Ponoroff, implacable, simply points to the signed contract, and says "A deal's a deal. Cough up the $50 or I'll sue."

Who's right? Ponoroff. A court would look at the skeletal agreement, and although sparse, would find enough there to think that the written expression contains all of the terms of the deal. Moreover, since the UCC governs Armie's sale, the applicable test would be whether if the collar were part of the deal, it "certainly" would have been included in the signed agreement. In this case, if the collar were part of the deal, the parties would have put it in writing (hey—it's a diamond studded collar, for crying out loud!). This is underscored by the presence of an integration clause. Such a clause makes it easy for the court to say that the written agreement contains all the terms because, in effect, that's what the integration clause says. In short, this is a completely integrated agreement, and Epstein was trying to introduce evidence of a prior agreement contrary to the parol evidence rule. He loses.

What if the written agreement didn't have the integration clause? That's a closer question; because now a court can't point to anything the parties signed indicating that the written expression of the agreement was complete. But the collar seems separate from Armie, and sufficiently different from Armie that a reasonable person would expect it to be mentioned in the written paper if it were to be included. On that reasoning, the court would conclude that the agreement is completely integrated and not allow Epstein to try to prove it as a term.

3. Exceptions

Are written agreements always so bulletproof? No. In fact, most of the time the issues related to parol evidence are issues about the exceptions to the rule. And there are many. If a party wants to show defenses of fraud or mistake, for example, there is an exception. It wouldn't be fair to handcuff a party to show fraud in the inducement, duress, or a mistake in formation. Say Markell signs a written contract to buy Armie for $1,000 from Epstein. When Epstein sues for breach, parol evidence will *not* prevent Markell from introducing evident that the only reason he signed was that Epstein was threatening to shoot Markell's dog if Markell didn't sign. In addition, if a party wants to show that an agreement is not completely integrated, there is an exception for that as well. For example, Ponoroff could introduce evidence that the simple signed paper that says "Armie for $25" and signed by both Epstein and Ponoroff didn't include the fact that Ponoroff could pay $5 a week for five weeks—the relative sparseness of the agreement lends credence to the claim that there were other terms.

There are, however, two exceptions that take up most of the discussion. The first is the ability of a party to show that there is an oral condition precedent to the effectiveness of an agreement. For example, say Epstein needs to borrow $10,000. Ponoroff will lend it, but only if Epstein puts up his ramshackle "shotgun shack," leftover from his Alabama days, as collateral for when Epstein (inevitably) defaults. To implement this, Epstein signs a deed to the house, and gives it to Ponoroff. The deed doesn't mention the loan and is complete on its face. Epstein and Ponoroff agree that Ponoroff won't record the deed so long as Epstein pays the loan on time.

But Ponoroff, mad at Epstein for his lateness on his contributions to this book, records the deed even though Epstein is current on the loan. Epstein contests this. Ponoroff invokes the parol evidence rule, pointing out that the deed is complete and doesn't mention the loan.

Epstein wins. He can successfully use the exception to the parol evidence rule to introduce evidence that there was an oral condition precedent to the effectiveness of the deed.

But the most important exception to the parol evidence rule is that, in some cases, parol evidence can be use to explain or provide the meaning of the written document, even if completely integrated. That is, you may be able to use external evidence—prior negotiations, dictionaries, letters between the parties—to assist in determining the meaning of (and likely, who is in breach of) a written contract.

Note how this is different from what we've discussed up to now. Before we were looking at the parties trying to show that the there were additional or supplement terms that weren't showing up in the writing. Now the parties agree on what writing contains the agreement; they just disagree on what it means.

But ambiguity is a slippery subject, causing generations of jurists to disagree on what it is, and when it is present. It is the subject of the next section after the overview.

4. Overview of Parol Evidence

Parol evidence can be analyzed using the "ICE" mnemonic. The letters stand for "*Integrated?*" "Completely Integrated" and "Exceptions" So:

First, *Integrated?* In order for the parol evidence rule to apply the agreement or one of its terms must be "integrated," that is, a final expression of the parties' agreement. This also means it has to be in writing. If it's integrated, prior terms are discharged and evidence which tends to establish those terms is irrelevant and the court will exclude it.

Second, *Completely* Integrated? Is the agreement completely integrated, that is, do all of the terms express the complete deal of the parties, or are some terms out, or for future discussion. Look for integration or merger clauses here. If the agreement is completely integrated, no prior agreements survive and the parties may not introduce evidence of additional or supplemental terms.

Finally, *Exceptions?* Even if the parol evidence rule applies, there may be exceptions. Is the party trying to introduce the evidence also alleging fraud in formation, or mistake? Are they trying to show that the agreement is not completely integrated? Or subject to an oral condition precedent? Or, as is most often the case, that some agreed term of the contract is ambiguous?

B. AMBIGUITY AND EXTERNAL EVIDENCE

Ambiguity matters only when competing understandings of a term lead to different duties. Most of the time, for example, the fact that "bank" can mean both a financial institution and the side of a river does not create confusion when "bank" is used in a contract. But sometimes common words can trip up the parties. This was the case with the word "chicken" in the famous case of *Frigaliment Importing Co., Ltd. v. B.N.S. International Sales Corp.*, a contracts casebook standard.

In that case, a New York seller contracted to sell "chicken" to a Swiss buyer. The Swiss thought they were getting young chickens suitable for broiling. The New York seller thought it could comply by delivering older, cheaper, chickens suitable for stewing. The price difference in the market between the two types, when compared to the contract price, was not such that either type was clearly indicated.

When the Swiss buyer sued the New York seller for delivering the older, tougher birds, the issue was joined, and the opinion runs through the various types of interpretive devices available to courts to sort this kind of mess out (we'll get to those in the next several sections). In the end, the Swiss buyer lost—not because the court found that "chicken" meant older stewing chicken—but because the Swiss buyer, as plaintiff, had the burden of proof of showing that, as used in the contract, "chicken" meant only younger broilers, and it had not carried that burden.

Frigaliment assumed that "chicken" was an ambiguous term. But what if the parties disagree on what is ambiguous? Two basic tests have been proposed; the "four-corners" or "plain meaning" test, and the "external evidence" test.

1. The Plain Meaning Rule vs. External Evidence Rule

Traditionally, courts have adopted a plain meaning rule. Under this rule, unless ambiguity can be shown from within the document itself—and without resort to external sources—then the parties cannot introduce evidence tending to show ambiguity. That is, unless the ambiguity arises and can be shown within the "four-corners" of the document, then a party could not introduce evidence of a meaning different that the accepted meaning of the term at issue.

For example, assume Ponoroff hires Epstein to "detail" his car for $150. They sign a contract, and Ponoroff gives the car to Epstein. The next day Epstein returns the car, still dirty, but with a detailed list of all its parts. When Ponoroff sues Epstein, Epstein seeks to show that in his business as a law professor, detailing means listing in exhaustive detail all component parts. Under a plain meaning view, Epstein's case will get tossed. The generally understood meaning of car "detailing" is to clean in great detail, and the court will use that meaning. Nothing in the contract would lead a reasonable person to take Epstein's viewpoint. As a result, parties in jurisdictions in which this rule prevails may usually introduce extrinsic evidence only when the contract is contradictory (different parts of the contract call for different delivery dates, for example), or when the terms are vague and have no accepted meaning.

Other courts are more flexible. They find ambiguity if a dispute word is capable of more than one meaning when viewed from the perspective of a reasonable person who understands the context of the contract and the relationship of the parties. Under the external evidence rule, parties may bring in evidence that is external or "extrinsic" to the contract in order to show ambiguity in more cases than under the plain meaning rule.

Take the following example. Epstein is an apiarist (fancy word for beekeeper). He likes bees and honey so much that he affectionately named his car "Honey." Ponoroff wants to buy it, and they agree on terms. The contract reads: "Ponoroff will buy Honey, and Epstein will sell Honey, for $1,000, delivery and payment next Tuesday at Epstein's house at noon. This paper contains all the terms of this deal." On Tuesday, Ponoroff shows up to find Epstein offering to deliver to Ponoroff $1,000 worth of bee's honey, not an automobile.

In a later suit for breach, Ponoroff arguably would be bound to take the honey in a plain meaning jurisdiction; the contract is not ambiguous on its face and Epstein's status as a seller of bee's honey tends to confirm the reasonableness of Epstein's position. (There might be some argument that "Honey" was initially capitalized indicating that it is a proper and not a collective noun, but ignore that distinction for now). In an external evidence jurisdiction, however, Ponoroff would prevail; he could show the ambiguity by introducing evidence of Epstein's name for his car, and of their negotiations.

The tension between these two viewpoints was the subject of Chief Judge Kozinski's opinion in *Trident Center v. Connecticut General Life Ins. Co.*—another case you might have seen in your casebook. In this case a law firm negotiated a loan with an insurance company. The note the law firm signed bore an interest rate of 12–1/4%, and had a prohibition on prepayment for twelve years; this provision protected the lender in case interest rates fell. And fall they did. The law firm then sued the insurance company, claiming that the twelve-year prohibition on repayment was "permitted" upon default, and subject only to a 10% fee. Rates had fallen so much that it would have been cheaper to refinance at the lower rate and pay the 10% fee, than keep paying the original payments. The law firm claimed to have extrinsic, or parol, evidence that such an interpretation was consistent with the parties' negotiations.

Judge Kozinski first found that the loan agreement was not reasonably susceptible to the law firm's interpretation. Under a plain meaning view, that would be the end of the matter. But Judge Kozinski was applying California law, and California law as he saw it required admission of extrinsic evidence regardless of how clear and unambiguous the contract (the note) was on its face. He thus reversed the district court's granting of a motion to dismiss— leaving open the possibility, however, that after allowing the extrinsic evidence to be proffered, the trial court could grant summary judgment if the proffered evidence did not overcome the clear words of the contract.

As you can see, the issue of what is "ambiguous" and what is "clear" often varies with the judge involved. The best strategy when presented with such questions is to first apply the plain meaning test—see if the document in which the alleged ambiguity exists has any contradictions or contrary uses of the term in question. If so, then you can use parol evidence. If not, then you cannot use evidence external to the contract to create the ambiguity. After this analysis, examine the alleged ambiguity through the lens of the context or "external evidence" test—inquire whether a reasonable person with the knowledge and experience of the parties would think the alleged ambiguity was genuine or spurious. If so, then the court will allow extrinsic evidence to clarify the term. If not, then you exclude the proffered parol evidence.

2. Interpretive Maxims

When presented with difficult questions of interpretation, courts will often resort to "maxims" of interpretation. These are short hand rules that distill cases and, in some cases, common sense, in an effort to figure out what the parties meant by the words they used. One main maxim is that a contract should be construed against its drafter—representing the notion that if someone drafted a less than perfect contract, then that person should bear the cost of ambiguity. Other maxims look to common sense. For example, generic terms will take the meaning from their context. (This rule often goes by its Latin name, *ejusdem generis*). A contract to sell, for example, the "horses, cattle, sheep and other animals" on a farm would likely include hogs on the farm, but not the seller's pet fish, or even her pet dog. And general wisdom holds that we should prefer an interpretation that leads to a valid contract, or one that furthers public policy, over an interpretation that produces invalid or illegal contracts.

3. Using the Parties Dealings to Remove Ambiguity—Course of Dealing and Course of Performance

In cases of confusion over contract terms, often the parties' actions speak louder than their words. In these cases, courts will look to how the parties actually acted with respect to similar or identical words in the contract, or in past dealings if they used similar contracts. If the performance arises within one contract, it is called "course of performance;" if prior similar contracts are used, it is called "course of dealing."

An example shows how these terms are applied. Epstein sells armadillos; Ponoroff buys them and resells them to specialty markets. Several years ago, Epstein and Ponoroff signed an armadillo sales contract that said: "All payments due on the 1st of the month following the month of sale." Since then, Epstein and Ponoroff have signed several similar contracts. Ponoroff has always paid on time, and when the 1st of the month was a weekend or holiday, he always paid on the next business day. Epstein never complained.

Recently, another armadillo buyer, Markell, has appeared on the scene and wants all the armadillos that he can buy, and he's willing to pay more than Ponoroff. Epstein has committed to sell to Ponoroff for the next three months on a contract containing the language above. The first of next month is on a Saturday; when Ponoroff tries to pay on Monday, Epstein tells Ponoroff he is late, and because of that breach, Epstein is canceling the contract. Ponoroff sues.

Ponoroff will win. He will show that there was a course of dealing between Ponoroff and Epstein over several years that interpreted the same language as giving Ponoroff until the first business day of the month to pay. He will also be able to show this evidence without running afoul of the parol evidence rule. Rather than supplementing or adding to the terms, he is showing how the parties are best understood to have meant the payment date term.

The same result follows if the contract is for six months, and Ponoroff has paid on the first business day for the first three months, and then Epstein pulls his stunt. In this case, not only would Ponoroff have the ability to show a course of dealing— consistent and accepted performance over several years of con- tracts–but also course of performance—consistent and accepted performance with respect to the very contract at issue.

4. Special Rules for Contracts of Adhesion

Parties often use preprinted forms, or economically powerful entities use their might to offer terms on a take-it-or-leave-it basis. These are examples of adhesion contracts—contracts in which there is no bargaining permitted and which offer no choice but to accept the terms as presented. Your apartment lease, your cell phone contract, a car rental contract are all examples of adhesion con- tracts. Make no mistake—**just because a contract is an adhe- sion contract does not mean it is unenforceable.**

To the contrary: most contracts in use are adhesion contracts, and the world gets along just fine. With contracts of adhesion, however, courts often will narrowly construe the terms in favor of the party who had no choice but to accept the terms offered. In some sense, this is a version of the legal maxim of construing the contract against the drafter, or of construing a contract so as to promote public policy. Most often these rules are used to construe insurance and other similar contracts in which a consumer pays for a standard service without the ability to bargain over much of anything.

A minority of jurisdictions adopt Section 211 of the *Restate- ment (Second)* on this point. It states that if a party attempting to enforce a particular provision of an adhesion contract knew, at formation, that the other party did not know of that particular provision's existence, and also had reason to believe that the other party would not have assented to the provision if they had known about it, then the court will delete the provision from the contract.

As an example, assume Epstein is the sole provider of bar exam tutoring services in Richmond (a sad, sad state of affairs were it true). He offers to tutor students, but only if they use his preprint- ed contract form. On the back of that form is a provision, in small,

8–point type and in light grey ink, that says "Upon passage of the bar, student agrees to give Epstein his or her first-born male son, or its financial equivalent, which the parties agree to be $10,000."

In jurisdictions adopting the *Restatement (Second)*, a court could initially find that the student didn't know about the provision, relying on its small and faint type, and its placement on the back of the contract. If the student shows that he or she would not have agreed to the provision had he or she known about it, then the court will delete the provision. Even in non-*Restatement* jurisdictions, a court might find the sale of an unborn child (or its pricing at $10,000) to be against public policy, and construe the contract as one against public policy, and not enforce it. Epstein, justifiably, loses.

C. IMPLIED TERMS

Even when a court can determine what the parties said or wrote, and what it means, that may not be the end of the analysis. Courts have long woven into existing contracts terms that the parties did not discuss or dicker over. These fall into two broad categories: terms implied by a court to achieve the parties intent, and terms implied to further some public policy.

1. Terms Implied to Achieve the Parties' Intent

People aren't perfect. Their written contracts don't always have all the terms they should. And some of these omissions might render the contract void or give the other party a technical basis to refuse performance. **Courts will thus provide missing terms when they are convinced that the parties intended to contract but overlooked or omitted an essential term that can be inferred from the circumstances.**

a. Obviously Omitted Terms

Such was the case in *Wood v. Lucy, Lady Duff–Gordon*; another casebook staple. In that case, Wood and Lucy had agreed that Wood would market Lucy's fashions. The problem was that while the contract spoke as to how to divide profits from their deal, and bound Lucy to an exclusive deal for a year, it did not contain Wood's promise to do anything. If true, then the contract would have been lacking consideration—and that was Lucy's argument when she breached the exclusivity provision of the deal, and when Wood sued.

Judge Cardozo found for Wood. He acknowledged that no specific provision bound Wood to do anything. But such a result, he argued, was senseless. The parties had obviously gone to great lengths to put in place a deal, even to the point of stating how the profits were to be split. Cardozo found that Wood's undertaking to use his reasonable efforts to make sales was "a promise ... fairly to be implied."

There is an obvious tension between cases like *Wood* and the "letter of intent" cases in which the parties don't agree to a deal, but merely specify the terms for further negotiations. In cases like *Wood*, however, courts can see that the parties intended a binding contract, and can specify with some precision the terms of the omitted provision.

b. Trade Usage

Often, the parties enter into a contract similar to contracts which lots of other people have entered into. For example, a broker buying farm produce, a person buying a home, or an employer hiring workers. These kinds of contracts are formed many times a day.

With such repetitive and common contracts, certain terms become refined and "old hat." When that happens, courts may imply them into contracts as "trade usage." That is, even though the parties may not have even thought about it, trade usage may insert terms into their contracts.

The UCC speaks of trade usage as "any practice or method of dealing having such regularity of observance in a place, vocation or trade as to justify an expectation that it will be observed with respect to the transaction in question." UCC § 1–303(c). Note how broad this is. It covers practices tied to a particular place, a particular job or vocation (such as plumbing), or a particular trade (homebuilding). Section 222 of the *Restatement (Second)* is essentially the same for contracts not governed by the UCC—essentially land contracts and contracts for services.

Take the sale of Armie that began this chapter. If the practice in the place where Epstein and Ponoroff live is to deliver a recent veterinarian's certificate with every armadillo sold, then that term is part of the deal even if not expressly agreed to by the parties. And Epstein can use parol evidence to show that it is a term of the deal. He is not supplementing or changing the deal; rather he is simply showing what the deal is.

Note that trade usage applies regardless of whether both parties are UCC 'merchants,' or regardless of whether they even know about the trade usage. The requirement of "such regularity of observance . . . as to justify an expectation" is sufficient to insert the usage into the contract. Thus, even if Ponoroff did not actually know of the trade custom, he is still bound to observe it, and is in breach if he tries to deliver Armie without the certificate.

2. Terms Implied to Achieve Policy Goals

Often courts and legislatures impose terms on contracting parties, even if the parties would not chose to include those terms if asked. The purpose of this practice is to ensure that all contracts meet certain public policy goals, or to ensure that default terms are provided to aid parties in the enforcement of their deals.

a. Implied Covenant of Good Faith and Fair Dealing

The main implied term is the implied covenant of good faith and fair dealing. Note that this is a term of a contract, and not a duty imposed, say, in negotiations for a contract. The content of this term is often fuzzy, but in essence it attempts to impose on parties the obligation to refrain from taking (or not taking) actions that would deprive the other party of the benefit of its bargain.

Say that Epstein hires Ponoroff to paint Epstein's picture. The contract says that the finished product "must be to Epstein's satisfaction" or Epstein doesn't have to pay. Epstein, seeing a way to get a free painting, suddenly adopts high standards of satisfaction, way beyond reasonable expectations. He rejects all of Ponoroff's efforts, even if they are excellent efforts to capture his grim visage. Here, a court would rule for Ponoroff if he sued for nonpayment. When the contract gave Epstein the power to exercise satisfaction, the law implied that he would exercise that discretion in good faith. Most courts interpret this as requiring honest satisfaction, measured most often by whether the satisfaction was reasonably (that is, objectively) exercised. Flat out rejection of all efforts would not qualify if Ponoroff's work would have been accepted by most people.

So too if a party's performance is subject to a condition that is in that party's control, the control must be exercised in good faith. If a party buying a house, for example, makes his or her purchase conditional on getting financing, or if a corporation makes an acquisition dependent on approval of its board of directors, then the buyer must actually attempt to obtain financing, and the corporation's board of directors must actually be presented with the proposal.

Many cases present conflicts between the express language of the contract and the implied covenant of good faith. In such cases, the express language will usually prevail. In the above example of Ponoroff's painting, if the contact had said "Epstein can exercise his discretion to express satisfaction capriciously or without explanation," then continuous rejection would not have violated the implied duty of good faith, since the parties' express understanding will control.

b.   UCC Supplied Terms

Finally, the UCC will actually supply "default" terms-gap filler provisions. That is, the UCC will insert into a contract various terms that might otherwise be thought to be terms necessary to form a definite contract. The UCC will, for example, provide the place of delivery (UCC § 2–308; seller's residence or place of business), and the time for performance (UCC § 2–309; a reasonable time). It may even insert a price (UCC § 2–305; a reasonable price, assuming the parties otherwise agreed to conclude their deal without agreeing to a price, which would occur if the object of the sale had a well-established market price).

If Epstein agrees to buy Armie from Ponoroff, but the contract doesn't specify a time or place, the UCC will insert these terms into the contract (Ponoroff's house, and a reasonable time). If they omit a price, however, a court will not insert a price term since armadillos are not subject to widely-quoted or accepted prices, and it would be difficult to hold that they intended to conclude a contract for such an animal without agreeing to a price.

Warranties form another important area of UCC-supplied terms. The implied warranty of title (a promise that the seller owns the goods sold) is one example. UCC § 2–312. Another is the implied warranty of merchantability. This is a promise inserted into the contract by the UCC that goods sold by a merchant will, among other things, be recognized in the trade as matching the contract description, be at least of fair average quality, and will be fit for the ordinary purposes for which such goods are used. UCC § 2–314. If Sally buys a toaster from an appliance store that blows up on first use, for example, then she has a claim for breach of the warranty of merchantability against the store even if the contract of sale says nothing about warranties.

Finally, all of these default terms can be, and often are, changed by terms the parties chose. This is usually indicated by language in the applicable UCC section that says something like "unless otherwise agreed." If Epstein and Ponoroff agree to deliver Armie in the middle of the night at 3:00 a.m., that is their prerogative, and no court will require a more reasonable time instead. More important, implied warranties are often excluded by express contract provisions. These contract provisions, commonly referred to as disclaimers, are covered by UCC § 2–010. If your professor covered § 2–316, then you need to re-read that provision.

Chapter 5

WHEN WILL PERFORMANCE OF THE DEAL BE EXCUSED?

Sometimes things happen after a contract is formed that excuse further contract performance. By "excuse" we mean that nonperformance of the promise is not considered a breach giving rise to liability. Because performance of promises is an important policy, the post-contract excuses are somewhat limited. In this chapter, we will review seven post-contract happenings that excuse further contract performance.

A. FIRST EXCUSE—OTHER GUY'S TOTAL NONPERFORMANCE

This one is easy. On Monday, Markell contracts to wash Ponoroff's car on Saturday for $10. Markell does not wash the car on Saturday. This is a "breach," a failure to perform a promise when due.

Obviously, Ponoroff does not have to pay Markell, i.e., Ponoroff is *excused* from paying (i.e. performing) because of Markell's prior nonperformance. And obviously, Ponoroff has a cause of action against Markell for breach of contract.

Too easy to be on your exam, but a base for us to build from.

B. SECOND EXCUSE—OTHER GUY'S SAYING HE IS NOT GOING TO PERFORM

Again, let' start with an easy example. On Monday, Markell contracts to wash Epstein's car for $10 on Saturday, with payment on Sunday. On Tuesday, Epstein calls Markell and tells him that he has changed his mind and will not pay Markell to wash the car on Saturday. Again, it should be obvious that Markell is excused from performing (i.e., washing the car) because of Epstein's saying he is not going to perform. And, again, it should be obvious that Markell has a cause of action against Epstein for breach of contract.

Epstein's unequivocally indicating that he is not going to perform is called repudiation. Because Epstein repudiated his contract performance obligation before it was time to perform, it is called anticipatory repudiation (or breach). **So you now know three things about anticipatory repudiation: (1) an anticipatory repudiation, if material, excuses further contract performance by the other guy just like in the case of an actual failure perform at the agreed upon time of performance, (2) an anticipatory repudiation is a form of breach of contract, and (3) anticipatory repudiation requires an unequivocal indication of intention not to performance; i.e., "absolutely declaring that he will never act under it."**

This quoted language is taken from *Hochster v. De La Tour*, the first "anticipatory repudiation case" in most casebooks. That case involved an April employment contract, with work to begin in June and repudiation by the employer on May 11. The employee/plaintiff sued on May 22 for breach of contract.

Hochster held that the employer's anticipatory repudiation gave the employee the option to sue immediately—i.e., that the employee did not have to wait until the June 1 contract performance date—for an actual breach—before bringing suit. This holding has been an important part of the law anticipatory repudiation.

It is also important to remember that in *Hochster* the *employer's anticipatory repudiation* left the employee free to take another job. This is not only consistent with the concept that anticipatory repudiation excuses further contract performance but also with the concept of avoidable damages, something we discuss in Chapter 6 below.

In *Hochster*, there was no dispute about the facts—no dispute about the employer's "absolutely declaring that he will never act under it." In other cases (and a number of law school exam problems), there are questions about what the facts are and whether the words and conduct of a contract party unequivocally indicate nonperformance. And the uncertainty about whether there has been an unequivocal indication of nonperformance by one party can cause the other party to anticipatorily repudiate by stopping his performance because he honestly but incorrectly believes that the other party has anticipatorily repudiated.

Assume, for example, that an employee believes that an employer's May communication absolutely declares that the employer will never perform their June contract and so the employee takes another job for the months of June and July. If the employer sued for breach of contract, and the court found that the employer's March communication was *not* an absolute declaration of its nonperformance, then the employee's taking another job was an anticipatory repudiation and a breach. In essence, if one party stops his performance because he honestly but incorrectly interprets the other party's post-contact words and conduct as rising to the level an anticipatory repudiation, then it is the first party who has actually committed the anticipatory repudiation .

C. THIRD EXCUSE—REASONABLE GROUNDS FOR INSECURITY

As the above example illustrates, sometimes the post-contract words and conduct are equivocal and so anticipatory repudiation is not available to excuse performance. Where such equivocal words or conduct by a buyer or a seller after a contract for a sale of goods give reasonable grounds for insecurity, then § 2–609 of the UCC provides a basis for excuse of further contract performance by the other party to the contract. More specifically, the other party can demand in writing adequate assurance of performance; (1) suspend her own performance until she receives adequate assurance, if commercially reasonable; and (ii) stop performance altogether if adequate assurance is not timely provided, without worrying that the stopping of performance might later be construed as a breach.

Assume for example that, in January, Ponoroff contracts with Epstein the boot maker for a pair of custom-made boots, with 25% of the purchase price to be paid by February 15, 25% of the purchase price paid on March 1, and the balance paid when the boots are delivered on March 15. On February 13, Ponoroff learns that Epstein was late on all of his January boot deliveries and that some of the boots Epstein delivered were poorly stitched. Under § 2–609, Ponoroff, with "reasonable grounds" for insecurity, could send Epstein a written demand for adequate assurance and "suspend" making payments until he received "adequate assurance."

In reading section § 2–609, you should notice the additional requirement of a written demand of adequate assurance and three possible litigable issues: (1) were there "reasonable grounds for insecurity", (2) was the assurance offered "adequate" and (3) was it "commercially reasonable" to suspend performance until receiving "adequate assurance." Similar language can be found in § 251 of the *Restatement (Second) of Contracts*.

D. FOURTH EXCUSE—OTHER GUY'S IMPROPER PERFORMANCE

The question of when one guy's improper performance excuses further contract performance from the other guy is a one of those questions that common law answers differently than UCC Article 2

Let's consider the common law answer first.

1. Common Law Material Breach Concept

While money damages can be recovered for any contract breach, only a *material* breach excuses further performance of a contract governed by common law. A material breach is, in essence, a major screw-up.

Whether a breach is "material" is a fact question and so it is unlikely that you will be asked to decide whether a breach is material unless it is obvious that there was a major screw-up. A breach can be material because of the quantity of performance (or lack thereof)—e.g., Ponoroff contracts to wash Markell's car and stops work after washing only the lower third of the car (have we mentioned that Ponoroff is short?) or because of the quality of performance (or lack thereof)—e.g., Ponoroff contracts to wash Markell's car and washes the entire car with a dirty chamois cloth so that the car is dirtier after Ponoroff finishes his performance than before he began.

In both of the above examples, the breach was obviously material. In the first case on material breach in most contracts casebooks, *Jacob & Youngs v. Kent*, the breach was obviously not material—at least to Judge Cardozo. The contract provided that all pipe in the house be wrought iron pipe manufactured by the Reading Pipe Co.; the builder instead used wrought iron pipe manufactured by the Cohoes Pipe Co. Judge Cardozo describes the breach as "both trivial and innocent." More important, he used the term "substantial performance."

It is important that you understand that if the performance is substantial, then the breach is not material and vice versa. There cannot be both substantial performance and material breach. And, so because there was substantial performance in *Jacob & Youngs v. Kent* and no material breach, the builder was successful in its suit to recover the balance of the purchase price—i.e., no material breach and so no excuse of the owner's payment obligations, subject to reduction for the damages caused by the minor breach.

There is important dictum in *Jacob & Youngs v. Kent*—"This is not to say that parties are not free by apt and certain words to effectuate a purpose the performance of every term shall be a condition of recovery." We will consider the quoted language when we consider conditions later in this chapter.

2. UCC Perfect Tender Concept

In a contract governed by Article 2 of the UCC, i.e., a sale of goods, the two parties are the buyer—who provides the money—and the seller—who provides the goods. And, the "improper performance" is almost always the seller's—a screw-up by the seller in what goods are delivered or how the goods are delivered. (Obviously there are Article 2 contract situations in which the buyer does not provide the money, but those situations involve non-performance, not "improper performance.")

Article 2 does not use the term "material breach." And, courts do not use the common law material breach concept in determining whether the seller's improper performance excuses the buyer from paying. Instead courts use the term "perfect tender," another term not used in the Uniform Commercial Code, in determining whether the seller's improper performance excuses the buyer from performing under § 2–601.

The statutory basis for the perfect tender rule is the following language in UCC § 2–601: "[I]f the goods or tender of delivery fail in any respect to conform to the contract, the buyer may * * * reject." And a buyer of goods who rightfully rejects the goods does not have to pay for the goods, i.e., she is excused from performing.

For example, if Markell, the seller, and Ponoroff contract for the sale of 1,000 green widgets for $100,000, and Markell delivers 999 green widgets and one yellow widget, Ponoroff can reject *all* of the widgets and does not have to pay Markell the $100,000. Because of the Uniform Commercial Code's perfect tender rule ("fail in any respect"), Markell's improper performance, albeit trivial, excuses Ponoroff from any performance obligation whatsoever.

This perfect tender rule is subject to a number of exceptions, such as § 2–508, which creates a right to cure and § 2–612, which suspends strict application of the perfect tender rule in the case of installment sales. Most contracts teachers leave coverage of these exceptions to commercial law courses and so will we.

E. FIFTH EXCUSE OF PERFORM-ANCE—NON-OCCURRENCE OF AN EXPRESS CONDITION

You need to know four things about express conditions: (i) what an express condition is, (ii) how an express condition is satisfied, (iii) when non-occurrence of an express condition is excused, and (iv) what the differences are between conditions precedent and conditions subsequent and between express conditions and constructive conditions.

1. What an Express Condition Is

And, there are three things to know about what an express condition is.

First, an express condition is language in a contract. If Markell offers to sell his house to Ponoroff and Ponoroff responds "I accept, conditioned on the house's being appraised at $200,000 or more," that response, as we learned in Chapter 2, is a conditional acceptance (or counteroffer). There is no contract and so no contract condition. In contrast, if Markell and Ponoroff enter into an agreement that states Ponoroff will buy and Markell will sell his house and that the sale is "conditioned on the house's being appraised at $200,000 or more," then we have a contract *and* an express condition. Again, we are looking for language in the contract itself.

Second, the language you are looking for in a contract is language that excuses the contract's other promises rather than creates new promises. The phrase "conditioned on the house's being appraised at $200,000 or more" is not a promise. Neither the seller, Markell, nor the buyer, Ponoroff, has promised that the house will be appraised at $200,000 or more. Neither the seller Markell nor the buyer Ponoroff can recover from the other for breach of contract if the house is appraised at less than $200,000. **Put simply, the failure to satisfy a condition is not a breach,** rather, the consequence of a less than $200,000 appraisal is that Ponoroff does not have to the buy the house; he is excused. As the title to this Part E indicates, nonoccurrence of an express condition excuses performance.

Third, while the cases and commentary consistently say that there are no magic words necessary for the existence of an express condition, there are magic words for you to watch for in exam hypotheticals. If you find the words "if," "only if," "provided that," "so long as," "subject to," "in the event that," "unless," "when," "until," and, of course, "on condition" in an exam question, then you are looking at a question on express conditions. If you don't see one of those phrases, then you need to understand that, whenever possible (and sometimes when it would seem impossible), courts will interpret the language as anything other than an express condition.

This preference for interpreting contract language as anything other than an express condition will become more understandable when you understand the answer to the second of the three things you need to know about express conditions—how is an express condition is satisfied?

2. How an Express Condition Is Satisfied

Don't let the language that the cases and commentary use confuse you. While it is the non-occurrence of an express condition that excuses performance, judges and law professors rarely use the language that "the express condition has occurred"; instead, look for the phrase "the condition has been satisfied." **If the express condition has been "satisfied," then there is no excuse of a later non-performance based on nonoccurrence of the express condition.**

And, generally, an express condition is "satisfied" only if it is complied with strictly. The first case on conditions in many casebooks, *Luttinger v. Rosen*, is a great illustration of the strict compliance concept. The contract was a home sale contract which like most home sale contracts, contained an express condition relating to financing a mortgage "from a bank or other lending institution * * * at an interest rate which does not exceed 8 ½ per cent per annum." While the lowest mortgage rate the buyers were offered by a bank was 8¾ per cent, the seller committed to fund the difference in interest payments. In the buyers' successful suit to recover their down payment, the court held that the buyers were excused from performance because the financing condition was not met. Even though the opinion does not use the term "strict compliance," judges and law professors cite *Luttinger* to support use of the strict compliance concept.

Test your understanding of the "strict compliance" concept by considering another home sale contract with an express condition. Change the facts of *Jacobs & Young v. Kent* so that the Kents' contract for Jacobs & Young to build their home provides in pertinent part that "the Kents payment obligations under this contract are expressly conditioned on Reading wrought iron pipe, and only Reading wrought iron pipe, being used throughout the house." Jacobs & Young instead uses Cohoes pipe. When the Kents refuse to pay for the house, Jacobs & Young sues for breach of contract. The court again finds that Jacobs & Young's use of Cohoes pipe was "innocent"; the court also again finds that the differences between Reading pipe and Cohoes pipe are "trivial."

Weren't the differences in *Luttinger* between a 8½ per cent mortgage interest rate and a 8¾ per cent mortgage interest rate with the sellers' paying the difference in the interest payments also trivial? In the hypothetical in the preceding paragraph, like in *Luttinger*, applying a strict compliance test means that the express condition in the contract is not satisfied—meaning that contract payment is excused. Is this what Judge Cardozo intended by his dictum in *Jacob & Youngs v. Kent*, "This is not to say that parties are not free by apt and certain words to effectuate the purpose that the performance of every term shall be a condition of recovery"?

Excusing the Kents from paying for a house that Jacobs & Young built for them because of the nonoccurrence of a condition seems more troublesome than excusing the Luttingers for paying for a house that Rosen was trying to sell. The *Restatement (Second)*, § 227 (cmt. b) uses the term "forfeiture" in describing the denial of payment because of the non-occurrence of a condition to someone, like Jacob & Youngs in our hypothetical who "relied substantially on the expectation of that exchange."

3. When Non-occurrence of a Condition Is Excused

Just as nature abhors a vacuum, courts abhor a forfeiture. Courts seek to avoid "forfeitures" by interpreting contract language as not imposing a condition, and also by excusing the non-occurrence of a condition when that non-occurrence of the condition would cause a disproportionate forfeiture. *Restatement (Second) of Contracts* § 229. And, the first of the illustrations accompanying § 229 is a hypothetical that looks very much like our hypothetical of *Jacob & Youngs* with language of express condition.

Restatement (Second) § 229 uses the verb phrase "may excuse." In other words, a court has discretion to excuse a condition to avoid a forfeiture. An exercise of that discretion involves a balancing of the policy of freedom of contract, on the one hand, and the policy of fairness, on the other. **So it is fair to say—though it sounds funny—that conditions may excuse performance, but the conditions may also be excused, in which the performance is due.**

Excuse of the non-occurrence of an express condition because of prevention or because of waiver is easier to understand.

Here is an example of excuse of the non-occurrence of an express condition under the doctrine of *prevention*: Markell contracts to buy an emerald pupik ring from Epstein for $10,000 on the condition that the ring is appraised at no less than $10,000. Markell later refuses to perform, i.e., pay Epstein the $10,000, because the appraised value was only $8,000. If Epstein can establish that Markell bribed the appraiser to provide a lower than market appraisal, then the non-occurrence of the express condition will be excused because of prevention (which is to say satisfaction of the condition was *prevented* from happening). And, the practical consequence of the excuse of the non-occurrence of the condition will be that either Markell pays the contract price for the ring or Epstein recovers damages from Markell for breach of contract.

More realistic, and more common, is excuse of the non-occurrence of an express condition because of waiver. Same pupik ring story except that (i) Markell does not bribe the appraiser, and (ii) Markell wants to buy the ring even though the condition was not satisfied because the appraiser valued the ring at $9,000. Obviously, Markell, the person protected by the condition, can give up (i.e., waive) the protection of the condition; Obviously, Epstein cannot use the non-occurrence of the appraisal condition as an excuse to refuse to sell the ring to Markell, since the condition governed Markell's performance (i.e., ran in his favor, not Epstein's).

4. Differences Between Express Conditions Precedent and Express Conditions Subsequent, and Between Express Conditions and Constructive Conditions

(a) Express conditions precedent

All of the preceding hypotheticals involve conditions precedent. **A condition is a condition precedent when it is a prerequisite to the parties' performance obligations.**

The adjective "precedent" refers to the time relationship between the occurrence of the express condition and the obligation to perform pursuant to the contract. The occurrence of the express condition—appraisal of the pupik ring at no less than $10,000—comes first, and "precedes" Markell's obligation to pay. Thus it is a condition precedent.

Most, if not all, the "condition cases" that you read will involve express conditions precedent.

(b) Express conditions subsequent

Contract language can also create an express condition *subsequent*. **A condition is a condition subsequent when it imposes a post-contractual limitation on the duty to perform.** For example, Spike Lee contracts to sell you his courtside, New York Knicks tickets for $10 a game until the New York Knicks are in first place. "Until the Knicks are in first place," like "on the condition that the pupik ring is appraised at no less than $10, 000," is an express condition. It is language in a contract that does not create a new obligation but rather limits a contract obligation otherwise created—Spike Lee's obligation to sell his Knicks tickets. Since the contract provides for Spike Lee's selling the tickets until the Knicks are in first place, i.e., the occurrence of the condition is subsequent to the performance, the condition is an express condition subsequent.

In summary, the primary practical difference between conditions precedent and conditions subsequent then is that the *non-occurrence* of a condition precedent excuses any contract performance, while the *occurrence* of a condition subsequent excuses continuing performance. Both the occurrence of express conditions precedent and the occurrence of express conditions subsequent are governed by the strict compliance rule. Spike Lee cannot use the Knicks' rising to second place as an excuse for his selling his courtside seats to you at $10 a game. Second is not "first." No strict compliance, no satisfaction of the express condition.

(c) Express conditions and constructive conditions

I do not cover constructive conditions in my contracts courses. I hope that your professor does not cover constructive conditions so that you can stop reading this subsection, but, if your professor is Ponoroff, you have to press on (a very small price to pay according to Ponoroff, if not his students).

It is easier to explain what constructive conditions are *not* than to explain what constructive conditions are. **Constructive conditions are not express conditions, not language in a contract that modifies obligations created by language of** promise in the contract, not subject to the strict compliance standard. Rather, constructive conditions are the language of promise in the contract and are subject to the material breach rule. Contract law developed the constructive condition concept to explain the first hypothetical in this chapter.

In case that hypothetical was not sufficiently memorable, "Markell contracts to wash Ponoroff's car on Saturday for $10. Markell does not wash the car." We said "Obviously, Ponoroff does not have to pay Markell."

As you will discover, if you mistakenly use the word "obviously" in one of your first year exam answers, "obviously" is not much of an explanation. A more complete explanation of why Ponoroff does not have to pay Markell is that Markell performing his contract obligations is viewed as a "constructive" condition to Ponoroff performing his contract obligations. ["Constructive" means made up by the court and not the parties.]

Regrettably, in the course of your contracts course you will read some early cases which use the term "condition" in discussing what is in substance a constructive condition, and some modern cases which use the term "condition" in discussing what is in substance an express condition. Worse, both early and modern cases refer to "breach of condition." While a constructive condition is in essence also a promise, and so can be breached, an express condition is not a promise and so cannot be breached. An express condition is either satisfied or not satisfied, and if it is not satisfied, there is an excuse of performance, but no breach. When *Luttinger* was unable to obtain the 8¼ mortgage, there was no breach—just an excuse from having to buy the Kleins' house.

In sum, constructive conditions of exchange is the doctrine developed in the 18th century to explain why the performance by each party to a contract is almost always dependent on the performance by the other contract party. If it were not for constructive (implied) conditions, then, in the above hypothetical, Ponoroff, who did not expressly condition his performance on Markell also performing, would have to pay Markell or be in breach himself, even though Markell did not do the work. Then he'd be forced to sue Markell to recover his $10, which makes no sense. So constructive conditions help to ensure that each party will receive the promised performance of the other party by making the respective promises mutually dependent on one another.

F.   SIXTH EXCUSE OF PERFORMANCE: IMPOSSIBILITY OR IMPRACTICABILITY

In the prior section on express conditions we dealt primarily with the effect of something not happening that the contract expressly contemplated happening—remember the Epstein/Markell pupik ring contract conditioned on the ring being appraised at no less than $10,000? In this section, we will be dealing primarily with the effect of something happening that the contract does *not* expressly contemplate.

Assume for example that after the Super Bowl was awarded to Richmond for 2017, Ponoroff contracted with Epstein to rent Epstein's Richmond home for the fourth week of January and the first week of February in 2017. Then, after the contract but a month before the Super Bowl, an unprecedented flood of the James River destroys Epstein's home. Should Epstein be excused from performing? Or instead, if after the contract but before the Super Bowl, Epstein dies? (Have we mentioned that Epstein is really old?) Or, instead, if after the contract but before the Super Bowl, the Commonwealth of Virginia enacts a law requiring that a person be at least 5 feet 7 inches tall to attend the Super Bowl? (Have we mentioned that Ponoroff is the "short" of this *Short and Happy* book?). In short (so to speak), what later occurrences, not anticipated by the contract, should excuse contract performance?

a.   Damage or destruction of the subject matter of the contract

1.   Common law

Most contracts casebooks include *Taylor v. Caldwell*. The subject matter of the contract that was destroyed was the Surrey Gardens, a music hall, owned by the defendant. The contract was a lease. The plaintiff, a concert promoter, leased the defendant's music hall for concerts on four separate days. After the lease contract but before any of the concerts, the concert hall burned to the ground. No one's fault—just another of life's little surprises. The promoter sued, claiming that the defendant had breached the contract by failing make Surrey Gardens available on the dates specified in the contract. The court held for the defendant, reasoning that the continued existence of the music hall was an "implied condition" of the lease, and concluding "performance becomes impossible from the perishing of the thing."

Today, courts, the *Restatement (Second) of Contracts* § 361, and law professors use the phrase "basic assumption," instead of "implied condition," and "Impracticable," instead of "impossible." But, it all pretty much means the same thing.

"Impracticable" is one of those words that you first encounter in law school You need to understand that while "impracticable" sounds more like "impractical" than "impossible," its meaning is more like impossible than impractical. Focus on the effect of the post-contract occurrence on the ability to perform.

Damage or destruction of the subject matter of the contract does not always excuse performance. Obviously, if Markell contracts to paint Epstein's house and the house burns down before Markell is finished, Markell is excused from performing. No ability to perform—nothing for the paint to stick to. By contrast, if Markell contracts to build a house for Epstein and the house burns down before Markell is finished; Markell is not excused from performing. Markell the house builder still has the ability to build the house.

Undoubtedly, it will now cost Markell more to build the house, but the performance becoming more expensive is generally different from the performance becoming impracticable. You will find dicta in cases and commentary to the effect that performance becomes impracticable when it can only be done at excessive and unreasonable cost but that is at best an outlier (and more important an unsatisfactory analysis for exam purposes).

2.   Uniform Commercial Code

In sale of goods cases, the question of whether destruction of the subject matter of the contract excuses performance only arises when goods "identified when the contract is made" have been damaged or destroyed. The nuances of what "identified" means is generally left for commercial law courses. For purposes of most contracts courses, it is sufficient to understand that:

- If Epstein contracts to sell Markell "my 1973 Cadillac" for $700 and before the car is tendered to Markell it is destroyed in a flood, Epstein's nonperformance is excused. The subject matter of the contract is Epstein's Cadillac and that has been destroyed. Markell cannot recover damages for breach of contract even if he can show that the market value of Epstein's Cadillac was $1,000.

- If Epstein contracts to sell Ponoroff 1,000 pounds of grits for $700 and all of Epstein's grits are destroyed in a flood, Epstein's nonperformance is not excused. No specific grits were "identified", and, happily, there are still a lot of grits in the world. Epstein can perform by buying more grits and reselling them to Ponoroff for $700. It may be that Epstein has to pay more than $700 for 1,000 pounds of grits, but again the performance becoming more expensive does not make performance impracticable

Obviously, the buyer's payment is also a subject matter of the contract. It should be equally obvious that destruction of the buyer's money is never going to be an excuse of nonperformance. Markell can't avoid the contract obligation of paying Epstein the contract price for the pupik ring even though Armie the armadillo ate all of Markell's money, which he was keeping in a box under his bed.

b.   Death of a Contract Party

Earlier, we considered the effect of a death of either the offeror or the offeree after the offer was made but before it was accepted. And we learned that death of either the offeror or the offeree terminates the offer.

But now we learn that death of either party to a contract after the contract was entered into, but before it is performed, does not generally terminate the contract. Unperformed contract obligations are generally not excused by death.

Assume for example that Ponoroff makes a loan to Epstein and before Epstein repays the loan he dies. Ponoroff can still recover the unpaid loan balance from Epstein's estate. Epstein's death does not excuse the repayment of the loan. If the law were otherwise, no one would extend credit to old people like Epstein.

The rule that death does not excuse performance is not limited to loan agreements. In theory, it applies to most contracts.

Assume Markell contracts with Ponoroff to paint Markell's house for $10,000 and then Ponoroff dies before he can get to the job. Markell is thus forced to find another painter, Epstein, to do the same job, but Epstein charges $13,000. On these facts, Markell should be able to recover $3,000 from Ponoroff's estate.

The contract in the preceding paragraph is viewed as a contract for a $10,000 paint job, not a contract for a paint job that could be performed only by Ponoroff. Admittedly, some (very few) contracts for personal services are treated differently. If, as in the dictum in *Taylor v. Caldwell*, the contract is for painter to paint a portrait instead of a house, then the contract might be viewed as one that could be performed only by that painter so that "in the case of a painter employed to paint a picture who is struck blind, it may be that performance might be excused." (Reconsider this paragraph when we consider in Chapter 7 the rule that contract performance obligations can generally be *delegated* from one person to another.)

We understand that, in the real world, people don't sue their painter's estate when the painter dies before finishing a painting contract. It is the kind of thing that only happens on law school exams.

c. Supervening Law or Regulation

This one is easy. Epstein contracts to sell Armie his pet armadillo to Markell. After the contract but before Epstein delivers or Markell pays, a law is enacted prohibiting the sale of armadillos. Obviously, performance is excused.

And what should also be obvious from this hypothetical is that **"legal" impossibility (or impracticability) is different from physical impossibility.** It was still physically possible for both parties to perform under the contract but performance was excused because it was not possible to perform without violating a supervening law.

d. Force Majeure and "Hell or High Water" Clauses

Ex payments for lease must continue irrespective of any difficulties paying party may encounter

Whether your professor wants you to use the term "impossibility" or the term "impracticability" or both, use these terms only when the facts involve a post-contract occurrence not provided for in the contract. Sometimes the contract provides for post-contract occurrences in either a force majeure clause that excuses performance in the event of a specified occurrence, or a hell or high water clause that requires performance regardless of what occurs.

You will probably see hell or high water clauses as part of your property course's treatment of landlord tenant law. If you see a force majeure clause on your contracts exam, apply its language, not the law of impossibility or impracticability, to the post-contract occurrence in the fact pattern.

G.   SEVENTH EXCUSE OF PERFORMANCE: FRUSTRATION OF PURPOSE

In the prior section on impossibility or impracticability as an excuse of contract performance, post-contract events not anticipated by the contract affected the ability to perform contract obligations. This section explores a similar but separate ground for excuse of contract performance—frustration of purpose. The doctrine of frustration of purpose is triggered by post-contract events not anticipated by the contract that do not affect the ability to perform, but instead affect the mutually understood *purpose* for the contract performance.

Krell v. Henry is the "frustration of purpose" case included in most contracts casebooks. Krell owned an apartment, 56A Pall Mall. The June 26 and June 27 coronation parades for Edward VII were scheduled to pass along Pall Mall, and Krell's apartment overlooked the parade route. Henry contracted for the daytime use of Krell's apartment for the days of the parades for a fee of £75 and paid £25 of the fee in advance. Because Edward suffered an appendicitis attack, the coronation was postponed. And, because the parades were postponed, Henry refused to pay the £50 balance of the fee. And because of Henry's refusal, Krell sued Henry for breach of contract to recover the £50.

Relying in part on *Taylor v. Caldwell,* the court held for the defendant Henry. You remember *Taylor v. Caldwell*—the case about the contract for the use of a concert hall that later was destroyed by fire. And, remembering the facts of *Taylor,* you can easily distinguish the facts of *Krell* from the facts of *Taylor.* Krell's flat was not destroyed (Indeed, as you will discover if you participate in Richmond's summer program in Cambridge, the flat is still standing today.) The cancellation of the parades had no effect on the ability to perform—Henry could have sat in Krell's flat on June 26 and June 27 and looked out the windows at a "parade less" Pall Mall. Rather, in *Krell v. Henry,* the cancellation of the parades affected the mutually understood purpose of the contract.

And, it is important that you understand that in *Krell v. Henry* both parties understood that viewing the coronation parades was the purpose of the contract. Krell had advertised that that his apartment had a view of the parades. Had that not been the case, the outcome would have been very different. *Restatement (Second)* § 265, entitled "Discharge By Supervening Frustration," adopts the *Krell v. Henry* result and uses the Krell fact pattern as the first

Illustration. Instead of the phrase "mutually understood purpose," § 265 uses the phrase "basic assumption."

Note also that § 265, like *Krell v. Henry*, only provides for the discharge of "remaining duties to render performance." In *Krell v. Henry*, Henry withdrew his counterclaim for the £25 that he had already paid, and that has become part of the modern doctrine.

Chapter 6

HOW DOES THE LAW ENFORCE THE DEAL (CONTRACT REMEDIES)?

A. OVERVIEW

When there is a breach of a contract, the law provides a remedy. Remedy here means something to compensate the non-breaching party for the consequences of the breaching party's actions. This is an area in which Contracts distinguishes itself from, say, Torts. Whereas Torts remedies are generally backward looking—putting the person in the position he or she was in before the injury—Contracts remedies are forward-looking. They seek to place the non-breaching party in the place he or she would have been in had there been performance.

Put another way, the law looks at what the non-breaching party reasonably expected, and fashions a remedy from that perspective. Colloquially put, the non-breaching party receives as a remedy the benefit of its bargain.[2] And usually, although not always, the amount of damages are determined without reference to the intent of the breaching party. Intentional breaches are generally treated the same as non-intentional ones.

2. This chapter looks at affirmative relief—money damages and specific performance—generally awarded after the parties have agreed the contract is over. There are also the remedies of suspension of performance, termination of the outstanding duties (the "executory" obligations), and rescission under the contract discussed in the prior chapter.

95

B. SPECIFIC PERFORMANCE

It might seem that the easiest way to award the benefit of the bargain would be to just order the breaching party to perform. If Epstein and Ponoroff agree that, in exchange for $1,000, Epstein will write Ponoroff's chapter in their casebook on Contracts, and Epstein is too drunk to perform, one might think that a court could order Epstein to sober up (good luck with that), and then perform. But for historical and sometimes constitutional reasons, American common law courts rarely resort to ordering a breaching party to do what it promised. Rather, courts will attempt to measure the loss incurred from the breach in money, and award damages.

There are, of course, exceptions. Courts may order "specific performance"—the buzz words for ordering the breaching party to do what was promised—when the remedy at law (damages) is inadequate to compensate and when it is fair and reasonable to compel performance. Note that there are two basic elements here: inadequate remedy; and "equity." Thus, if Ponoroff wants specific performance from a sobered-up Epstein in the contract above, a court might not grant it even if Ponoroff's damage remedy is inadequate. It may be that the value of such a chapter is $100,000 (hah!), and the enforcement on such a sharp bargain would be inequitable. It may be that what constitutes an acceptable chapter is too uncertain to be enforced, or that such an order would be too difficult to police and enforce (hard to keep Epstein away from the bottle). It also may be—as is the case with many personal service contracts—that enforcement could run afoul of the constitutional ban on involuntary servitude (although not likely here, since not all of Epstein's life would be bound up in performance).

Most cases, however, focus on the inadequacy of the remedy at law. Compressed, this inquiry is one into whether money will adequately compensate. Where the contract involves the sale of a unique, or presumed unique item, inadequacy is presumed. In this category are contracts for the sale of land, but can also include rare and irreplaceable items of personal property, such as famous paintings, highly customized and rare cars, unique handmade clocks, and the like. Thus, if Ponoroff agrees to sell "Desert Doozy," his palatial decanal residence, to Epstein for $100,000, and then breaches, Epstein will likely be able to contend that his remedies at law are inadequate, since land is unique. A court will then enter a decree of specific performance requiring Ponoroff to convey Desert Doozy to Epstein.

Assume that, instead of selling his house, Ponoroff agreed with Epstein that Epstein would publish all of Ponoroff's academic writings for a specified royalty. Assume that this is not an illusory promise, and also assume Ponoroff starts publishing his writings with Markell in breach of these obligations. Epstein's remedy at law is likely inadequate; Ponoroff's work product is certainly unique and not capable of precise measurement of worth. But a court might not want to order Ponoroff to perform, for all the supervisory and equitable reasons mentioned above. In such cases, a court is likely to enter a "negative injunction." Under this remedy, the court will order Ponoroff *not* to publish with anybody but Epstein. Thus, Ponoroff isn't forced to work for Epstein, but he can't profit by selling to Markell, or anyone else for that matter.

But most contracts don't deal with unique subjects. Assume that Ponoroff and Epstein agree that Ponoroff will sell his pet armadillo, Armie, to Epstein for $35. Armie, although an affectionate armadillo, isn't unique. You can buy armadillos at specialty pet stores for $50 and up. When Ponoroff develops an unusual attachment to Armie at the last moment, and refuses to deliver him to Epstein, can Epstein obtain specific performance? No. Epstein's remedy at law is not inadequate; Armie isn't unique, and as we will see in the next section, Epstein has a perfectly fine remedy at law: damages.

C. NAMES FOR DAMAGES

Before looking at the how to calculate contractual damages, it is helpful to look at the names courts put on damages for purposes of discussion. Be aware, however, that courts (and law professors) use lots of different names for damages, and they aren't always consistent.

1. Direct or General

"Direct" or "general" damages are the type usually discussed. They are the type of damages necessary to award the non-breaching party the benefit of his or her bargain. Thus, in the armadillo sale example above, $15 would compensate Epstein for Ponoroff's failure to sell Armie (Epstein expected to buy an armadillo worth $50 for $35, so he is damages to the extent to the shortfall, or $15). These $15 would be direct damages.

2. Special or Consequential

But what if Epstein needed Armie because he had agreed to resell—or flip—Armie to Markell for $300 (assume Markell had taken an irrational liking to Armie). Ponoroff's breach meant that Epstein lost out on profit on resale. Epstein could claim that his inability to collect the $300 from Markell was an indirect or special consequence of Ponoroff's breach. And in a way, he would be correct. To put Epstein in the position he would have been in had Ponoroff not breached, Epstein's damage award should include not only his direct damages of $15, but also an amount equal to his lost profit on his flip sale to Markell (which would equal $250). We call this type of damage, usually dependent on particular or special circumstances surrounding the non-breaching party, "indirect" or "special" damages. The UCC, some cases and some contracts professors use the term "consequential damages." UCC § 2–715(2). The bottom line is that, although some try to make reasoned distinctions, there is little if any difference between the usages of "indirect damages," "special damages," or "consequential damages."

Sometimes it is difficult to tell what is direct and what is indirect, or what is general and what is special. Generally, the more particular the damages are to the non-breaching party—a special, second, contract to sell goods once obtained, or a relatively narrow use only applicable to the non-breaching party—the more likely they are to be special damages.

3. Incidental

Incidental damages are those costs necessary to respond to or correct a breach. In the sale of Armie on page 97, if Epstein has to make a long distance call to get a replacement for Armie, the cost of that call is incidental to that breach and compensable as incidental damages. In general, the costs of obtaining substitute performance (getting another armadillo in the above example) are incidental damages.

There is a major limitation on incidental damages. The American Rule states that attorneys' fees, unless otherwise contracted for or provided by statute, are not recoverable as incidental damages. So if Epstein incurs $1,000 bill from attorney Markell in order to sue Ponoroff for failure to deliver Armie, that $1,000 is not recoverable as incidental damages. That would change, and Epstein would get the $1,000, only if the contract provided for attorneys' fees.[3]

D. GENERAL MEASURE OF MONEY DAMAGES

America's common law system prefers money damages as a remedy. In other words, courts will value the loss occasioned by the

---

3. There are also nominal damages, which are usually a small amount—$1 or $10 is typical—used to signal that there has been a breach but no provable damages.

breach, and substitute that value as a damage remedy. As a result, most contracts remedies questions explore the calculation of these damages.

1.   Benefit of Bargain—The Expectation Interest

As indicated in the opening of this chapter, Contract law protects the parties' expectation interests; that is, it protects what the parties reasonably expected to obtain by full performance of the contract. This is often expressed as the effort to put the non-breaching party in as good a position as he or she would have been in had the contract been performed.

It is important to understand what this means. Assume that Epstein and Markell agree that Epstein will wash Markell's car for $10, when the cost of a similar wash is $25. Also assume that five minutes after making this contract, Epstein says to Markell: "You know the car wash? Forget it. I don't know what I was thinking. And since you didn't pay me anything to seal the deal, I'm not paying you one cent in damages." One might say that Markell isn't harmed at all. Epstein is right (a rarity): Markell didn't pay Epstein anything, and Markell's in the same position he was in only a scant six minutes earlier. No harm, no foul, right?

Wrong. Contracts law says that even though Markell didn't pay Epstein a dime, he is still harmed. The formation of a contract also carried with it the formation of a reasonable expectation of getting a service for $10 that would otherwise cost $25. Thus, when Epstein breaches, he owes Markell the benefit of Markell's bargain. As we will see, this turns out to be $15, or the difference between what Markell will have to pay someone else—$25—to do what Epstein promised to do for $10.

2.   Ways to Measure Benefit of Bargain—Difference in Value of Performance

Much of contracts remedies is figuring out how to measure the benefit of the bargain. In the car wash example, we picked the difference between the value of what was promised ($10) and the value of what the service was worth ($25). The concept is that the party should not get the full amount of what they had to pay to secure the performance lost by the breach; that would overcompensate because inherent in the deal was that Markell was going to pay $10 in any case. He just gets money damages for the extra $15 he didn't expect to pay.

This measure of damages was used in the famous "hairy hand" case of *Hawkins v. McGee*. There, Hawkins had burned his hand. His doctor, McGee, "guaranteed" (a fancy word for promised) that he would make the hand a "one hundred percent good hand." He didn't. His surgical technique of grafting skin wound up not only failing to fix the hand, but making it worse. It grew hair.

The issue was how to measure the damage. The court excluded pain and suffering since that was going to occur in any case (much like Markell having to pay $10 in the prior example). The court elected to treat the guaranty of a good hand as a "warranty" (another fancy word for promise), and awarded damages on the following formula: Hawkins would be entitled to damages equal to the difference between the value of the hand as promised (a "one hundred percent good hand") and the value of the hand as delivered (a hairy, deformed, hand). The case doesn't tell us what those damages were.

This measure of damages is often used without any change when the object of the contract has a value can be determined without reference to the contract. Put another way, it is often used when there is a market for what was to be bought and sold under the contract, or if there is some way to independently determine the value of the object "as promised." Obviously, if there is a market for the kind of object mentioned in the contract, proof of what the market would charge would also be proof of what the value of the promise was.

To see this, assume Epstein agrees to sell to Markell Grade A maple syrup. Epstein breach and instead delivers Grade B. If Markell discovers the difference only after delivery, which is reasonable, can he use the Grade B syrup and still obtain damages? Yes. Following the general rule in *Hawkins*, he can get the difference in price between Grade A and Grade B. If the contract called for 1,000 gallons of syrup and Grade A sold for $1 a gallon and Grade B sold for $.75 a gallon, the damages would be $250, or the product of 1,000 times the price differential of $.25.

In cases of delayed performance, as opposed to failure to perform, the value of performance due can also be measured by awarding interest on the value of the property or the rental value of the delay. So if Epstein did deliver Grade syrup in the above example, but did so a week late, Markell's damages could be interest on the value of the syrup for a week. If interest were 10% per year, the damages would be 10% times the value of the syrup, $1,000, for one week (or $1.92, which is $100 divided by 52 weeks).

3. Ways to Measure Benefit of Bargain—Cost of Repair or Completion

Sometimes, especially in building contracts, it is difficult to calculate the value as delivered, especially when the builder breaches before completion of the project. In those cases, courts will often take the cost of completion as a substitute measure for the difference in value approach. For example, if Epstein agrees with Ponoroff to build a mansion for Ponoroff for $1,000,000, which Ponoroff foolishly pays for before Epstein ever shows up to start the job. Epstein walks off the job half way through. Ponoroff has to spend another $500,000 to complete the project. Here, Ponoroff's damages will be $500,000, the cost to complete the job. That is what is required to put Ponoroff in the position he would have been in had Epstein not breached.

Things can get messy under this formula if there have been progress payments instead of a lump sum up front payment. In the prior example, assume that Ponoroff had paid only $250,000 up front to Epstein, but still paid just $500,000 to finish the house. In this case, no damages! Why? Ponoroff wound up paying only $750,000 for a house he expected to pay $1,000,000 for. If, instead, Ponoroff had to pay the substitute builder $1,000,000, his damages would be $250,000: he wound up paying $1,250,000 for a house he agreed with Epstein should cost only $1,000,000.

The notion here is that the ultimate value of what is contracted for is reasonably related to the cost of building or completing it. That is, the specs for Ponoroff's house were really for a house that would have a value somewhere in the neighborhood of $1,000,000. But what if that assumption is wrong? Assume that Ponoroff's specs called for the brazen exploitation of the University of Arizona logos in every conceivable place, to the point of the faucets in the bathrooms being in the shape of "A" and "U"? Put another way, what if the million dollar cost produces a hundred thousand dollar house?

4. Limitation on Cost of Repair or Completion—Economic Waste

With some difficulty, courts have sometimes limited the cost of completion remedy by not awarding it if it would result in damages disproportionate to the likely loss. That is, if the cost of completion is more than the value of the object when built or as promised, courts fall back to the *Hawkins* type remedy and require the non-breaching party to prove the difference between what was contracted for and what was delivered. In this calculation, courts analyze what it would cost to give full performance, and what the value of the property involved would be after that performance.

This was the issue faced in two leading cases, *Groves v. John Wunder Co.* and *Peevyhouse v. Garland Coal & Mining Co.* In *Groves*, a property owner leased land to another with the understanding that the lessee could remove sand and gravel from the property during the term of the lease. The lessee also agreed to restore the property back to its original state. It didn't. It contended that it would cost $60,000 to restore the property, and that after such restoration the property would be worth only $12,160. In *Peevyhouse*, there was a similar lease, but the lease allowed the lessee to remove coal instead of sand and gravel. The cost of restoring the property in *Peevyhouse* was $29,000; after that expenditure, the property would increase in value by $300.

Groves gave damages of $60,000; *Peevyhouse* only $300. *Peevyhouse* probably better represents the *Restatement* and majority view that the cost of completing performance is limited if that cost is clearly disproportionate to the probable loss in value. Sometimes, as in *Groves*, the court will award higher damages if the breach was intentional, but this is contrary to the notion that the amount of damages will not vary with the type of breach.

E. LIMITATIONS ON DAMAGES

Once the potential to award consequential or special damages is recognized, then contracts damages can be greatly expanded to cover any loss than might have been caused by a breach. Contract law limits damages, however, in ways that require additional showings by non-breaching parties. **Damages have to be certain, foreseeable, and unavoidable. The last limitation—unavoidability—covers both post-breach costs that should not have been incurred and post-breach opportunities that should have been pursued.**

1. Certainty

One of the major limitations on damages is certainty. **Contract damages must be proved to a reasonable certainty, a standard higher than that typically used, for example, in Torts.** For most contract breaches this will not be much of an issue. If Epstein breaches a contract to sell 10 copies of his bankruptcy casebook, the price of the casebook can be established to a reasonable certainty. Markets exist to give that price. As a consequence, the typical situation in which the certainty requirement restricts damages is when the non-breaching party wants lost profits as part of his or her damages. **To be compensable, lost profits must be shown with reasonable certainty.**

As an example, assume Ponoroff wants to buy Epstein's theater so that his acting company, Ponoroff's Players, can put on plays for profit. They sign a contract that calls for Ponoroff to pay market price for the theater. Epstein breaches, and Ponoroff buys another theater for the same price, but closes on it a month later. Ponoroff has no direct damages, because the price for the substitute theater was market price. There is no difference between the contract price and the price Ponoroff had to pay for a different theater. At most, Ponoroff has some incidental damages related to obtaining a different theater for his company.

But in the meantime, Ponoroff's Players have no place to act. They can't put on shows, and can't earn any money. Ponoroff is out the profits his company would make during this time. In short, to give Ponoroff the benefit of his bargain—that is, to put him in a place equivalent to where he would have been had Epstein performed—Epstein should pay Ponoroff an amount equal to Ponoroff's lost profits.

But contract law will require Ponoroff to show these lost profits with reasonable certainty. As a practical matter, if Ponoroff's Players is a new company with no operating history, Ponoroff will not be able to show lost profits under this standard. New ventures rarely can show profits with any certainty. If Ponoroff's Players are an established company with a good track record, however, Ponoroff might be able to meet the standard. He can show that in the past, under similar circumstances, he has made a profit, and that Epstein's breach caused this trend to end.

2. Foreseeability

Another major limitation on damages is foreseeability. This limitation applies primarily to special or consequential damages. The classic case establishing this doctrine is *Hadley v. Baxendale*, an 1854 case from England. In this case, a miller sent an essential piece of his millworks—a driveshaft—out for repair. It apparently was the mill's only shaft, and the mill could not operate without it. The company transporting the shaft delayed its transport to the extent that there was a breach of the contract to transport. The miller asked for damages not only for the delay in transport—something like the difference FedEx charges for overnight and two-day delivery—but also for its lost profits for the time the mill had to shut down.

The court denied the lost profits. It imposed what has been called the foreseeability limitation: damages are recoverable only to the extent that the breaching party, at the time of contract formation, could reasonably have foreseen the loss its breach ultimately caused. In *Hadley*, although the case's preliminary material indicates that the transport company was told that the mill would have to shut down until the shaft was returned, the case itself says that all the breaching transport company knew was that their customers were millers, and that they were transporting a mill shaft. There apparently was no communication of the fact that the mill would have to shut down until return of the shaft; the transport company could, apparently, assume that the millers had a spare that they were using in the interim.

As a result, to be charged with consequential or special damages, the breaching party must have been able, at the time of contract formation, to reasonably have foreseen the loss its breach could ultimately cause. This knowledge comes generally from two sources. Either it is made known during the formation process, and therefore written into the contract, or the general circumstances of the object of the contract or the parties must reasonably known to all.

Take the following example. Epstein agrees to sell his comic book collection to Markell for $1,000, a reasonable estimate of the collection's market price. Without telling Epstein, Markell had already entered into a contract to flip the collection and sell it to Ponoroff for $1,100. If Epstein breaches, Markell has no damages other than perhaps incidental damages. The contract was for the market price, and thus his expectation for direct damages has not been harmed. When Markell tries to recover the $100 lost profits on his sale to Ponoroff, Epstein will be able to successfully defend on the basis that it was not reasonably foreseeable that Markell would flip the collection. For all Epstein knew, Markell was just another collector.

The result would change if Epstein and everybody else knew that Markell was not a collector, but just an opportunistic comic book broker who only bought comic books he knew he could immediately resell. This changed fact means that Epstein knew that Markell was not buying to hold or for personal reasons; he was buying solely to resell. Markell's lost profits on any resale of the comic books would thus be foreseeable to Epstein. He thus enters into the contract with knowledge that any breach by him could foil a resale—and damage Markell in the amount of profits related to that resale. In this latter case, then, Epstein is liable to Markell for the $100.

[handwritten margin note: No thin-skull Ts in contracts.]

3. Avoidability—Mitigation and Costs You Don't Have to Pay

A third limitation on damages is avoidability. There are two basic forms of avoidability. The first, called "mitigation," is usually represented by situations in which the non-breaching party could obtain substitute performance and minimize his or her loss. The second type of avoidability is when, because of the breach, the non-breaching party does not have to pay for his or her return performance.

The first type of avoidability, and the one most casebooks focus on, is usually called mitigation. **The mitigation principle denies damages to the non-breaching party if the damages were avoidable if only the non-breaching party had obtained substitute performance.** Often confusingly referred to as a "duty to mitigate," it is really a causation issue. **Breaching parties are not liable for damages that the non-breaching party could have avoided.** There is no duty—primarily because failure to mitigate does not give rise to any cause of action—but rather a break in the chain of causation.

Mitigation issues usually arise when the non-breaching party has opportunities to lessen the damages caused by the breach by obtaining alternate or substitute performance, and declines to exercise those options thereby compounding, rather than cutting, his losses. If Ponoroff breaches a lease agreement by leaving two years before the end of the lease's term, Ponoroff would generally be liable to the landlord for two years' worth of rent. But if Ponoroff can show—because it will be his burden—that the landlord could have re-let the premises one month after he left for the same rent, Ponoroff is only liable for one month's rent. Put another way, if a non-breaching party can mitigate—or lessen—the amount of damages, he or she must do so or risk not recovering all damages.

There are limits to mitigation. A non-breaching party does not have to mitigate if to do so would require undue risk, burden or humiliation. This often arises in employment contracts. An example would be as follows: assume Ponoroff signs a contract with Epstein to hire Epstein for a three-month summer associate position at $3,000 per month. On the first day Epstein reports to work, Ponoroff realizes what a big mistake he has made and fires him on the spot. Epstein can't get a summer associate position anywhere at that late date, and sues Ponoroff for $9,000. Ponoroff defends, pointing out that there were plenty of minimum wage jobs available to Epstein at $1,200 a month, which he chose not to take. As a result, Ponoroff argues that he isn't responsible for Epstein's lack of a job.

Epstein wins. A person is not required to take any job to mitigate. It must be of the same general type, involving the same general duties. Although fun for all, the vision of Epstein flipping burgers is likely humiliating (and less humiliating than Epstein as a summer associate). As a result, Epstein is not required to take any job to preserve his claim against Ponoroff.

While mitigation deals with avoidable damages, the second type of avoidability focuses on not awarding avoidable costs. Avoidable cost issues arise most often in contracts which require the non-breaching party to make partial payments or to make deliveries of products to the other before completion of the project. If there is a breach before completion, the doctrine of avoidable costs will not allow the non-breaching party to recover damages related to the buying or providing what the non-breaching party was to purchase or deliver under the contract. The breach made such expenditures avoidable, and thus incurring them should not result in additional damages.

This is illustrated by the following. Epstein signs a contract with Ponoroff to sculpt a statute of Ponoroff out of plaster of paris, delivery in six weeks. Ponoroff is to supply the plaster of paris. After signing the contract, but before actually starting work—and before Ponoroff buys the plaster of paris—Epstein breaches and walks off the job. Ponoroff can recover his general measure of damages (which may be the cost of completion), but what he can't recover is the cost of the plaster of paris that would have been required to complete the job. Once Epstein walked off the job, Ponoroff had the opportunity to avoid incurring the additional cost. Since he did not take advantage of that opportunity to avoid the cost, the cost cannot be charged to Epstein.

4. No Emotional Distress or Punitive Damages

Another distinction between Contract and other types of damages is that contract damages do not include damages for emotional distress (unless such distress was serious, and clearly foreseeable at formation—as if Ponoroff's Funeral Parlor agrees with Markell for burial services for Markell's grandmother, and then neglects to put the body in the casket before burial). Contract law also does not award punitive damages—damages designed to deter future similar conduct or to punish conduct.

F. LIQUIDATED DAMAGES

Contract law is the law of consensual obligation, so parties ought to be able to junk all of the above and design their own measure of damages, right? Wrong. **Although the law permits and tolerates the parties to set the amount of damages for breach—sometimes called liquidated damages since the clauses set, or "liquidate" the amount, and sometimes called agreed damages—it does so with certain key limitations.**

The basic limitation is that the amount of liquidated damages cannot do more than compensate. This is usually expressed as the fact that liquidated damages may not impose a penalty. Along this line, the first limitation is that the amount set must be difficult to determine. Damages that are easy to calculate—such as breach of delivery for generally available items with well-established markets like commodities or shares of traded stock—cannot be subject to enforceable liquidated damages clauses. Since compensation is easy to determine in these cases, the presumption of a penalty grows along with the ease of determination. Why would a party set damages in advance if damages can be easily calculated after breach?

Even when the damages are difficult to determine, the contemporary view is that the amount set must also be reasonable in light of the anticipated *or actual loss. Restatement (Second) § 256.* This means that there are at least two points in time which you must consider: the time of formation, and the time of breach. This also means that a clause which sets an unreasonable amount in light of what parties think at the time of formation may later prove to be reasonable if circumstances change drastically, and the damages set are reasonable in light of actual loss. Also, keep in mind that the penalty aspect can occur if the damages are set too low as well as if they are set too high.

At earlier common law, the rule was that the reasonableness of the amount set as liquidated damages was determined at the time the contract was entered into. This meant that if the stipulated sum was not a reasonable forecast of actual damages, the provision could be struck even if it turned to be reasonable in light of the actual loss. Under either the older or modern view as to when "reasonableness" is measured, the rule that this factor is satisfied when the amount set is deemed to be reasonable in light of anticipated loss (as of the time the contract was entered) is put to the test when actual damages turn out to be zero. Courts are split on this one.

An example illustrates some of these points. Assume that Epstein and Ponoroff sign a contract in which Epstein will tutor Ponoroff in Contracts at $100 per session. The fine print contains a clause that says that if Ponoroff breaches by not showing up within five minutes of a scheduled appointment, he owes Epstein $500 in liquidated damages for the breach. Regardless of whether damages may be easily determined, this clause is unreasonable—It provides for damages in an amount five times greater than the maximum that Epstein could expect under the contract's terms for that session.

Tougher questions arise when contracts set "fees" or other amount for breach. Take your mobile phone contract. It undoubtedly contains a clause that says you pay a fee of over a $100 if you terminate your contract early. Even if couched as a fee, this is a liquidated damages clause. Your early termination is a breach of your agreement to be a customer for a certain time. But what are the damages if you breach? Well, the company loses your monthly billings, but also doesn't have to provide you with monthly service. It also may lose other business opportunities tied to the number of subscribers it has. It thus meets the first requirement that the damages be difficult to determine. Whether the amount is reasonable either at formation or at breach requirement more study as to what losses the provider suffers when it loses customers.

Note that there is a direct link between the requirement of difficulty in determining damages and the requirement of certainty in damages. When parties anticipate that damages from the other side's breach might result in damages that will be difficult to quantify, they may very well decide to insert a provision for liquidated damages so that they can avoid that factual dispute in the event of breach. Similarly, if the damages would be mostly in lost profits—as in a new business' supply contracts with its vendors—a liquidated damage clause is often used to assure some compensation upon breach by the vendors.

G. RELIANCE AND RESTITUTION DAMAGES AS ALTERNATIVES

In many cases, a breaching party will not be able to show that its damages are certain or were foreseeable. In these cases, Contract law will often not leave the breaching party without any damages. Instead of awarding damages based on the expectation interest, the court will award damages based on the reliance interest. In such cases, courts look to out-of-pocket costs or other similar costs that the non-breaching party incurred in reliance on the contract. Put another way, in these cases, the court will look to the value of amounts spent by the non-breaching party in reliance on receiving performance under the contract from the breaching party.

Assume that Ponoroff agrees to sell his empty diner to Epstein, and Epstein arranges for financing and buys materials necessary to bring the diner up to code. If Ponoroff breaches before conveying the diner to Epstein, Epstein might say that his damages are his future lost profits from running the diner (his road-kill armadillo is just delicious). But as explored above, future lost profits for a new business are rarely certain enough to be awarded as damages. In the alternative, a court will give Epstein his out-of-pocket costs, such as the cost of his financing and the cost in buying the materials to fix up the diner.

Sometimes a court will award damages equal to a party's restitution interest. This interest is not keyed to what the non-breaching party spent, but rather to the value of the performance up until breach. It often arises when a party disaffirms or avoids a contract, or when, after some performance, the parties' remaining duties are discharged by impracticability or impossibility.

This is illustrated by the following. Assume that Epstein signs a contract with Markell under which Markell will buy land from Epstein for $100,000. Unbeknownst to Markell, Epstein misrepresented material facts to Markell, and those misrepresentations would allow Markell to avoid the contract. A year later, after Markell spends $10,000 making improvements to the property, he discovers the fraud, and seeks to avoid the contract. Markell will not only get back his $100,000, but will also receive the value of his improvements; if they are worth $15,000 ($5,000 more than he paid), he will receive his original $100,000 plus the value of the improvements, or another $15,000. He, of course, will have to return the land to Epstein.

A similar result would occur if Markell agreed to pay $100,000 for the property, paying $10,000 at signing, and agreeing to pay $90,000 at closing. If before closing the property is destroyed by a tornado to such an extent that both parties duties are discharged under the doctrine of impracticability, Markell has an action in restitution to a refund of his $10,000 that he paid notwithstanding that all other duties under the contract have been discharged.

H. UCC CHANGES TO DAMAGES

The UCC makes some subtle changes to damages. While a buyer may still recover the difference between the market price of the goods the seller agreed to sell and the contract price, the UCC makes proof of damages somewhat easier. Rather than having to prove market price, which would require an expert to opine on what the market was, the buyer can purchase substitute goods and recover the difference between the substitution cost and the contract price. Section 2–712 of the UCC calls this "cover," and conditions its use on the repurchase being in good faith, without unreasonable delay, and at reasonable terms. Thus, if Epstein breaches his contract to sell Ponoroff Armie the armadillo for $10, and then Ponoroff promptly buys a substitute armadillo for $25, his damages will be set by that price—$25—if it was in good faith and otherwise reasonable.

The concept of cover also factors in recovery of consequential damages. Section 2–715 conditions the recovery of consequential damages (usually lost profits on a resale of the goods or something to be built with the goods) not only on foreseeability, but also on the fact that the loss by the non-breaching party "could not reasonably be prevented by cover or otherwise."

Sellers' damages also change under the UCC. If a buyer simply refuses to take delivery, a seller may resell the goods in good faith and in a commercially reasonable manner and use the resale price as a proxy or substitute for the market price of the goods. UCC § 2–706. If he cannot resell the goods, the seller can recover the contract price and keep the goods (although if he sells them, the buyer gets a credit for the sale price). UCC § 2–709.

Finally, UCC § 2–708(2) allows for special damages for the "volume seller." The issue arises when a seller is in the business of selling multiple similar items, such as a car dealership for cars, or a jet plane manufacturer. The argument could be made that when a buyer breaches a contract to buy a car, for example, the dealer is not damaged because he can get someone else to buy the same car. The UCC rejects this position for volume sellers, finding that these sellers are damaged in such circumstances. Thus, a seller can recover the lost profits on a lost sale. This doesn't apply to situations in which the seller is limited to selling goods on hand, or otherwise has limits on his capacity. In these cases, the regular measure of damages adequately compensates the seller for each lost sale.

This is illustrated by the following. Assume that Epstein sells used cars. Ponoroff and Epstein agree that Ponoroff will buy a car for $1,000. Epstein's profit on the sale will be $250. If Ponoroff breaches by refusing to take delivery, Epstein can recover $250 from Ponoroff even if Epstein sells the car Ponoroff wanted the next day for $1,100. An exception would exist if Epstein had every other car on the lot under contract, and obtained a replacement sale after Ponoroff's breach. In that case, he wasn't really damaged by Ponoroff's breach, as he still gets a profit on every car on the lot, and giving him damages for Ponoroff's breach would unjustly enrich Epstein by the amount of the profit on the car Ponoroff wanted to buy.

I. CONTRACTUAL LIMITATION ON DAMAGES

Contracts being contracts, parties can agree to limit or even eliminate damages. We saw that initially with respect to the section on liquidated damages. But the parties can go further. They can change the type of remedy from money damages to some sort of alternate performance. Contracts in which manufacturers of consumer goods state that the exclusive remedy in case of a breakage while under warranty is an agreement to "repair or replace" the goods are one such example. Other examples include contracts which limit the remedy to a return of the purchase price. A different type of restriction allows parties to eliminate entire classes of damages. It is not unusual, for example, for a party to exclude consequential damages from a contract; FedEx, harkening back to *Hadley v. Baxendale*, excludes consequential damages from their contracts.

Under the UCC and to a lesser extent the common law, limitation of damage clauses are not enforced when the exclusive or limited remedy "fails of its essential purpose." § 2–719(2). This can occur, for example, if a television seller repeatedly fails to fix a television, and becomes clear that the seller can't or won't fix it within a reasonable time. If a court won't enforce the limitation or exclusive remedy, the parties go back to the general remedies given by the UCC.

Exclusion or limitation of consequential damages is likewise permitted unless the exclusion or limitation would be unconscionable. Under the UCC, for example, limiting or excluding consequential damages for personal injury in the sale of consumer goods is prima facie unconscionable. UCC § 2–719(3).

Chapter 7

WHO ELSE IS AFFECTED BY THE DEAL? (THIRD PARTY INTERESTS)

Sometimes a contract between two people affects the rights and duties of some third person who did not enter into (and was not party to) that contract. This can be done in two basic ways:

1. A and B make a contract intending to benefit C, creating a *third party beneficiary*; or

2. A and B make a contract. Later, either A or B (i) transfers its rights under that contract to C, making an *assignment;* or (ii) transfers its duties to C, making a *delegation or*;(iii)transfers both its rights and its duties to C, making both an *assignment* and a *delegation.*

A.   THIRD PARTY BENEFICIARIES

You need to know three things about third party beneficiary law: (1) what is a third party beneficiary contract, (2) what is the vocabulary of third party beneficiary law, (3) when do the rights of a third party beneficiary vest?

1.   What Is a Third Party Beneficiary Contact?

Looking at the most common form of third party beneficiary contract, a life insurance contract, is the easiest way to understand what a third party beneficiary contract is. Say Epstein signs up with Allfarm Insurance Co. for a $25,000 life insurance policy. That is a contract between Epstein and Allfarm. Epstein promises to make annual premium payments of $1,000, and Allfarm promises to pay $25,000 in policy benefits to Sharon Stone upon Epstein's death. Everyone understands that when Epstein dies, Sharon Stone has a legal right to collect the $25,000 from Allfarm.

Sharon Stone has that legal right to recover under the Epstein/Allfarm insurance contract even though she was not in "privity" with Allfarm and even though she did not provide any consideration. And, Sharon Stone's right to recover from Allfarm under the Epstein/Allfarm insurance contract is based on general contract law principles, not some special rule for life insurance policies.

Consider *Lawrence v. Fox,* the third party beneficiary case that appears in most contracts casebooks. Holly owed Lawrence $300. Holly then enters into a contract with Fox in which Fox, for consideration, promises to pay $300 to Lawrence. Again, the contract in question was between Holly and Fox. Although Lawrence was not a party to that contract, and was not the source of the consideration to Fox, Lawrence had a contract law right to recover the $300. Holly and Fox made their contract to benefit (pay) Lawrence.

2. What Is the Vocabulary of Third Party Beneficiary Law?

There are seven vocabulary terms that your professor (or the cases that your professor asks you to read) might use in discussing third party beneficiary law.

(1) **"third party beneficiary"**—This one is easy. Sharon Stone is the third party beneficiary (TPB) of the Epstein/Allfarm contract, and Lawrence is the TPB of the Holly/Fox contract.

(2) **"promisor"**—Harder, because each party to a contract makes a promise to the other. For example, Epstein is promising to pay insurance premiums to Allfarm, and Allfarm is promising Epstein that it will pay policy benefits to Sharon Stone. While both Epstein and Allfarm are making promises, only one is called the "promisor" in third beneficiary "talk." And, in third party beneficiary talk, the "promisor" is Allfarm—the person whose promise most directly benefits the third party beneficiary. Similarly, in *Lawrence v. Fox*, Fox, the person who promised Holly that he would make the payment to Lawrence, would be the promisor.

(3) **"promisee"**—Only person left, the other person who made the contract. Epstein is a "promisee." Holly is a promisee.

(4) **"intended beneficiary"**—The term is self-descriptive. Sharon Stone is an "intended beneficiary" because Epstein and Allfarm intended for her to benefit from the insurance contact. Or, in the language of R2k section 302, "recognition of a right to performance in the beneficiary ("Sharon Stone") is appropriate to effectuate the intent of the parties ... "

(5) **"incidental beneficiary"**—Less helpful is the *Restatement (Second) of Contracts* § 302(2) definition of an incidental beneficiary: "An incidental beneficiary is a beneficiary who is not an intended beneficiary." Here is an illustrative hypothetical: Apple contracts to buy Ponoroff's land to build a Mac Superstore. Ponoroff's land is adjacent to Epstein's family farm. Epstein would benefit from the performance of the contract between Apple and Ponoroff. Epstein's benefitting was not, however, the intent of the parties—not something that Apple and Ponoroff were thinking about when they contracted. Epstein's benefitting from the enhanced value of his family farm was just sort of incidental to the contract. Epstein would be an incidental beneficiary.

And, as Epstein is an incidental beneficiary of the Apple/Ponoroff contract, neither Apple nor Ponoroff would have any contract law duties to Epstein, and so Epstein has no rights under the contract. Only an intended beneficiary has contract law rights.

Understandably (at least we hope that you understand why), whether a person is an intended beneficiary or an incidental beneficiary is the most frequently litigated third party beneficiary question. In the real world, the answer to the question of whether a third party is an intended or an incidental beneficiary turns on what the parties to the contract intended at the time of the contract. On your exam, the grade for your answer to the question of whether a third party is an intended or incidental beneficiary will turn on your effectiveness in (i) comparing the facts in the exam question with the facts of the cases you've studied and (ii) using words you can spell.

(6) **"donee beneficiary"** and (7) **"creditor beneficiary"**—Under the vocabulary of the first *Restatement* and

many courts and law professors today, any intended beneficiary will be either a donee beneficiary or a creditor beneficiary. And, the third party is usually a donee beneficiary
unless (i) the promisee was, prior to the contract, indebted
to the third party beneficiary, and (ii) the contract performance satisfies that debt. Lawrence is an example of a
creditor beneficiary. (Remember, Holly, the promisee, owed
Lawrence $300). On the other hand, under the facts of the
Epstein/Allfarm hypothetical, Sharon Stone is a donee beneficiary. Today, whether a third party beneficiary is a
"donee beneficiary" or "creditor beneficiary" is of limited
practical significance. What is important is determining
whether the beneficiary is "intended" or "incidental," and
both a "donee beneficiary" and a "creditor beneficiary"
are "intended beneficiaries."

3.   Have the Rights of the Third Beneficiary Vested?

Determining when the rights of the third party beneficiary
have vested can also be important. Vesting can be important
because it has long been the "law" that once the rights of the third
party beneficiary "vest," the promisor and promisee cannot modify
or eliminate those rights. What has changed through the years is
the "law" of when the rights of a third party beneficiary vest.
Restatement (Second) § 311 probably reflects the present majority
rule that the rights of a third party beneficiary vest if, before being
notified of any modification or cancellation of his contract rights, he
either "materially changes his position in justifiable reliance on the
promise or brings suit on it or manifests assent to it at the request
of either the promisor or the promisee."

Assume, for example, that Markell enters into a contract with
Epstein that provides that Markell will pay Epstein $100, and
Epstein will deliver his armadillo, Armie, to Ponoroff. Ponoroff
learns of this contract, and, in reliance on Epstein's promise to
deliver Armie to him, Ponoroff gives his pet cats to Carl Gallagher
(everyone knows cats and armadillos do not peacefully co-exist,
although Markell and Ponoroff have no clue as to who Carl Gallagher is). Under these facts, Ponoroff's rights have vested. And,
under third party beneficiary law, Ponoroff, as an intended third
party beneficiary whose rights have vested, could enforce the contract between Epstein and Markell, even though he was not a party
to that contract.

B. ASSIGNMENT

A second way that a third party gains rights under a contract that she was not party to is through *assignment*.

You need to know three things about assignments: (1) what is an assignment, (2) what is assignment vocabulary, and (3) what are the limitations on assignments?

1. What Is an Assignment?

An assignment involves two separate transactions. First, two people make a contract. Then, later, in a separate transaction, one of the two parties to that contract transfers its rights under that contract to somebody else.

Contracts create rights in both parties to the contract. If Epstein contracts with Markell to sell his armadillo, Armie, to Markell for $10, with both payment and delivery of Armie to occur next Saturday at Epstein's office, Epstein has a right to the $10 on delivery of Armie and Markell has a right to Armie on payment of the $10. [Ponoroff insists that we add that this is another example of the operation of constructive conditions that we discussed back in Chapter 5.]

Either party to a contract can later transfer its contractual rights to a third party through *assignment*. So, if in our hypothetical, the next day, Markell gives or sells Ponoroff the right to Armie, then Markell has *assigned* his contract right. Even though Ponoroff was not party to the original contract, Ponoroff, not Markell, now has the contract right to take delivery of Armie in Epstein's office on Saturday. Notice that assignee Ponoroff has that contract right even if he did not provide consideration to Markell for the assignment. Just as there can be donee third party beneficiaries, there can be gratuitous assignees.

If Epstein decides that his life would have no meaning without Armie and breaches, assignee Ponoroff can sue Epstein's pants off, but assignor Markell cannot. This makes sense, because an assignment means that Markell has transferred his contract rights to Ponoroff.

2. What Is Assignment Vocabulary?

In our hypothetical, Markell is the "assignor," Ponoroff is the "assignee," and Epstein is the "obligor." The "assignor" is thus the party to the contract who later transfers his rights under the contract to someone else. The "assignee" is that someone else. And, the obligor is the other party to the contract—Epstein, the person who originally owed a contract duty to the assignor Markell, but now, as a result of the assignment, owes that contract duty to assignee Ponoroff, some third party with whom Epstein did not contract.

3. What Are the Limitations on Assignments?

Generally, most contract rights can be assigned. The primary common law limitation on the power to assign contractual rights is that an assignment cannot "materially change the duty of the obligor." *See Restatement (Second) of Contracts* § 317(2)(a). While the determination of whether an assignment is a material change is a fact question, to get the gist of it, compare the following two assignments:

(1) ***Assignment of right to services***: Ponoroff and Markell make a contract where Ponoroff is to pay Markell $15 dollars to wash his car. After the contract but before performance, Ponoroff assigns his right to a clean car to Epstein. Epstein, an old person, has an old person's car, a 1972 Cadillac. http://anticupid.org/1972–cadilac.html. Ponoroff, a short person, has a short person's car, a Fiat Cinquecento http://www.fiatusa.com/en/500/exterior/.

(2) ***Assignment of a right to payment***: Same original contract, but Markell, not Ponoroff, is the assignor. Markell assigns his right to the $15 payment to Epstein.

People who have seen both a 1972 Cadillac and Fiat Cinquecento would agree that it is harder to wash a 1972 Cadillac than a Fiat 500, and so, assignment (1) materially changes Markell's duty. Thus the assignment Case (1) is not effective. By contrast, it is no harder for Ponoroff to pay $15 to assignee Epstein than to pay $15 to assignor Markell. The assignment in Case (2) does not involve a material change in obligor Ponoroff's duty. Thus, assignment (2) is effective.

Generally, most contract rights *can* be assigned even if the contract states that contract rights *cannot* be assigned. Because of the policy against restraints on alienation of property,[4] courts strain to interpret anti-assignment provisions as limiting the "right" to assign, but not the "power"

---

4. Even though you learn about contract rights in Contracts and not Property, contract rights are property.

to assign. To understand this distinction, compare the following two contract provisions:

(1) Language of invalidation: Ponoroff rents an apartment from Epstein. The contract provides, "Assignments without the consent of the landlord Epstein are null and void." Ponoroff nonetheless assigns the right to occupy the apartment to Markell.

(2) Language of prohibition: Ponoroff rents an apartment from Epstein. The contract provides, "Assignments without the consent of the landlord Epstein are prohibited." Ponoroff nonetheless assigns the right to occupy the apartment to Markell.

Unless other circumstances indicate the contrary, most courts would hold that in Case (1) the assignment is not effective, and thus, Markell has no right to occupy the apartment. Contract provisions that expressly address the effect of an assignment—contract phrases such as "assignments are null and void," "assignments will have no force or effect" or "assignments will be disregarded"—prevent assignments.

By contrast, unless other circumstances indicate the contrary, most courts would hold that in Case (2), the assignment is effective, and so Markell has the right to occupy the apartment. This is because in Case (2), unlike Case (1), the contract language merely says "don't assign" without expressly addressing what happens if there is an assignment. In Case (2), therefore, the assignment would be legal, notwithstanding the anti-assignment provision in the lease contract, meaning that Markell could occupy the apartment. Ponoroff has the power to assign. He did not, however, have the *authority* to do so because prohibited his right to assign unilaterally. Therefore, Epstein must suffer Markell as a tenant, but he has a claim for damages measured by any economic loss that he sustains because Markell is occupying the apartment instead of Ponoroff.

C. DELEGATION

You need to know four things about delegation: (1) what is a delegation, (2) what is the delegation vocabulary, (3) what are the legal consequences of a delegation, and (4) what are the legal limits on delegation?

1. What Is a Delegation?

Contracts create not only rights but also duties. Each party to a contract has both rights and also duties. If Markell contracts to wash Ponoroff's car for $15, Markell has not only a contract *right* to be paid $15 for washing Ponoroff's car, but also the contract *duty* to perform the service of washing Ponoroff's car. If, in Tom Sawyer-like fashion, Markell convinces Epstein to wash Ponoroff's car, that is a delegation of Markell's duty.

If Markell induces Epstein to wash Ponoroff's car by telling Epstein that Epstein can collect the $15 that would be *both* a delegation and assignment. In the real world, transactions that are both assignments and delegations are more common than a transaction that is only an assignment or only a delegation. In the unreal world of law school exams, you are more likely to see a transaction that is only a delegation. And, even if the exam transaction is both an assignment and a delegation, exam issues are likely to be delegation issues.

2.   What Is Delegation Vocabulary?

The person who first makes a contract and then finds someone else to do his work under the contract is called the "delegator" or the "delegating party," and that "someone else" is the "delegatee." In the preceding paragraph's car wash hypothetical, Markell is the "delegating party" and Epstein is the "delegatee." Ponoroff, the other party to the contract—the person who has a right to the car wash—is the "obligee."

3.   What Are the Legal Consequences of a Delegation?

There are two possible *factual* outcomes from a delegation.

The first possible factual outcome from a delegation is that the delegatee performs. For example, you hire Ponoroff to paint your house for $100. Ponoroff delegates the obligation to Markell, who does a great job of painting your house.

The *legal* consequences of delegatee Markell's painting your house and doing a great job is exactly the same as if there had been no delegation and the delegating party Ponoroff had painted your house. Ponoroff's contract duties are discharged, and (unless Ponoroff had made an assignment as well as a delegation) Ponoroff now has a contract right to recover the $100 from you.

The other possible *factual* outcome from a delegation is that the delegatee breaches by either not performing or performing improperly. After Ponoroff delegates to Markell the contract duty to paint your house, Markell breaches by either not painting your house or doing a bad job of painting your house.

The *legal* consequence of nonperformance or improper performance by the delegatee Markell is exactly the same as the legal consequences if there had been no delegation and the delegating party, Ponoroff, had breached. You can sue Ponoroff; he is the one who promised you that your house would be painted, and there has been a breach.

In sum, the mere act of delegation does not absolve the delegating party of its contract duty. Rather, absolution of the delegating party requires both the delegation and then proper performance by the delegatee.

Now let's focus on the legal consequences of a delegation on the delegatee. Whether you, the obligee, can also sue delegatee Markell if he does not properly perform delegated duties requires more facts and a review of the concepts of (i) consideration and (ii) third party beneficiary. Recall that not all promises are legally enforceable; to be legally enforceable, a promise must be supported by consideration or a consideration substitute.

If in our house-painting hypothetical, Markell promised that he would paint your house because Ponoroff had promised to pay Markell $90, then Markell's promise would be legally enforceable. It was supported by consideration. And you would be able to enforce Markell's promise, even though it was in exchange for a promise from Ponoroff, because you would be the third party beneficiary of that delegation agreement between Markell and Ponoroff. Correspondingly, if the delegation was not supported by consideration, then Markell's promise to paint your house is not enforceable either by you, as third party beneficiary or by Ponoroff, the delegating party.

4. What Are the Legal Limits on Delegations?

Most contract duties can be delegated. The general rule that contract duties can be delegated is somewhat counter-intuitive and inconsistent with common expectations. You expect that when you contract with Ponoroff to paint your house for $100 that Ponoroff will do the painting. Yet, as we have seen in the preceding paragraphs, if Ponoroff delegates that duty to Markell, and Markell does a great job (or even just an acceptable, non-material breach kind of job) of painting your house, then Ponoroff's contract duties to you have been discharged and Ponoroff has a contract right to be paid the $100.

This general rule that contract duties can be delegated may seem more reasonable if you also remember from the preceding paragraphs the legal consequences of a delegation followed by a less-than-proper contract performance by the delegatee. If Ponoroff delegates that duty to paint your house to Markell, and Markell does not do a great job of painting your house, then you still have contract rights against Ponoroff.

The general rule that contract duties can be delegated becomes even more reasonable when you learn the two exceptions to that rule.

The first exception to the general rule that contract duties are delegable is what we call the "contract language exception." If your contract with Ponoroff provides that he cannot delegate his contract duty to paint your house, then you don't have to accept performance from anyone else. When Markell shows up to paint your house, introducing himself as "Markell the delegatee," you can tell him to "hit the road" and that you want the short guy with whom you contracted to paint your house.

And, under the language of both *Restatement (Second)* § 322 and UCC § 2–210, contract language prohibiting "assignments" also bars delegation.

In a sense, then, the rule that contract duties are delegable is a "default rule." It only applies if the parties have not inserted a contract provision relating to delegations or assignments.

The second exception to the general rule that contract duties are delegable is what some courts call a "personal services" exception. You will find statements in cases that duties to provide personal services cannot be delegated. However, even the courts that use the term "personal services" emphasize the word "personal" and limit the "personal services" exception to services contract in which the discretion, reputation, or skill of the person who contracts to perform the services is important to the other contract party.

Both the *Restatement (Second)* and the Uniform Commercial Code recognize a similar exception to the general rule that contract duties can be delegated by using different words. Under *Restatement (Second)* § 318 and UCC § 2–210, a contract duty cannot be delegated if the other party to the contract has a "substantial interest" in having that person perform.

To illustrate this exception, suppose your contract with Ponoroff was not to have your house painted, but to have your portrait painted. Ponoroff is a famous portrait painter whose style is particularly pleasing to you. It stands to reason that Ponoroff could not delegate this contract duty to Markell, an ordinary housepainter, without your consent. The same holds true even if Markell is a renowned portrait painter himself because you were bargaining for Ponoroff's personal performance when entering into this contract and no one else's.

Whether your Prof calls this exception a "personal services" exception or a "substantial interest" exception, determination of whether the exception applies so that the obligee can refuse performance by the delegatee is fact specific and basically a judgment call on which reasonable people can differ. For example, your three authors differ on the answer to the following hypothetical. West contracts with Epstein to write a contracts treatise, and Epstein attempts to delegate that duty to Markell and Ponoroff. Can obligee West still insist on performance by Epstein?

LAST WORDS

As promised by the words on the cover, this book is "short." And, since you are on this page, you are now "happy." Happy that you are through with this book; happy that you now understand the law of contracts.

Because we want you to be happy when you receive your contracts grade, we need to emphasize another word on the cover of this book—"Guide." This book is not a treatise, not even a hornbook, not even a concise hornbook, not even a nutshell, not even . . . .

In other words, to insure your "A" in contracts, you need to look at some other words. Most important, the words of your prof. You can find these words in your notes—assuming you regularly attend class. Or better yet, the notes of that conscientious person sitting next you who did not realize that the best way of making it through boring contracts classes was by listening to Gogol Bordello on You Tube.

Your prof might have some different ideas from ours as to what is important. Your prof might even have some different ideas from ours as to what the law is.

Obviously, we are right and your prof is wrong. And, obviously that is not what is important. What is important is that your prof is one that grades your exam. So, your prof has the last words.

We genuinely hope this book has helped, because, even if not, we have no intention of giving you a refund. As Epstein's Aunt Gertrude would say, "A contract is a contract, is a contract."

DGE
BAM
LP